Essays and Studies 1997

The English Association

The objects of the English Association are to promote the knowledge and appreciation of the English language and its literature, and to foster good practice in its teaching and learning at all levels.

The Association pursues these aims by creating opportunities of co-operation among all those interested in English; by furthering the recognition of English as essential in education; by discussing methods of English teaching; by holding lectures, conferences, and other meetings; by publishing journals, books, and leaflets; and by forming local branches.

Publications

The Year's Work in English Studies. An annual bibliography. Published by Blackwell.

The Year's Work in Critical and Cultural Theory. An annual bibliography. Published by Blackwell.

Essays and Studies. An annual volume of essays by various scholars assembled by the collector covering usually a wide range of subjects and authors from the medieval to the modern. Published by D.S. Brewer.

English. A journal of the Association, *English* is published three times a year by the Association.

The Use of English. A journal of the Association, *The Use of English* is published three times a year by the Association.

Newsletter. A *Newsletter* is published three times a year giving information about forthcoming publications, conferences, and other matters of interest.

Benefits of Membership

Institutional Membership

Full members receive copies of *The Year's Work in English Studies, Essays and Studies, English* (3 issues) and three *Newsletters.*

Ordinary Membership covers *English* (3 issues) and three *Newsletters.*

Schools Membership includes copies of each issue of *English* and *The Use of English*, one copy of *Essays and Studies*, three *Newsletters*, and preferential booking and rates for various conferences held by the Association.

Individual Membership

Individuals take out Basic Membership, which entitles them to buy all regular publications of the English Association at a discounted price, and attend Association gatherings.

For further details write to The Secretary, The English Association, The University of Leicester, University Road, Leicester, LE1 7RH.

Essays and Studies 1997

Translating Literature

Edited by
Susan Bassnett

for the English Association

D. S. BREWER

PR13.E5 n.s. v.50 1997

ESSAYS AND STUDIES 1997
IS VOLUME FIFTY IN THE NEW SERIES
OF ESSAYS AND STUDIES COLLECTED ON BEHALF OF
THE ENGLISH ASSOCIATION
ISSN 0071–1357

First published 1997
D. S. Brewer, Cambridge

D. S. Brewer is an imprint of Boydell & Brewer Ltd
PO Box 9, Woodbridge, Suffolk IP12 3DF, UK
and of Boydell & Brewer Inc.
PO Box 41026, Rochester NY 14604–4126, USA

ISBN 0 85991 522 0

A catalogue record for this book is available
from the British Library

The Library of Congress has cataloged this serial publication:
Catalog card number 36–8431

This book is printed on acid-free paper

Printed in Great Britain by
St Edmundsbury Press Ltd, Bury St Edmunds, Suffolk

Contents

Intricate Pathways:
Observations on Translation and Literature

SUSAN BASSNETT

IN HIS STORY, 'Pierre Menard, Author of the Quixote', Borges recounts how a twentieth-century writer decides to write Cervantes' *Don Quixote* anew. He proposes to rewrite the novel word for word, though he is quite clear that what he wants to accomplish is something entirely new:

> He did not want to compose another *Quixote* – which is easy – but the *Quixote itself*. Needless to say, he never contemplated a mechanical transcription of the original; he did not propose to copy it. His admirable intention was to produce a few pages which would coincide – word for word and line for line – with those of Miguel de Cervantes.[1]

He sets to work systematically, learning sixteenth-century Spanish, getting himself captured by the Moors, losing an arm and in every detail recreating the life Cervantes lived, for without total recreation he cannot fulfill his task. By the end of the story he has succeeded, and he has produced a text that is identical to the original *Don Quixote*. The narrator then comments on Menard's version, arguing that his version is more subtle than Cervantes' and is ultimately a better work.

Borges satirizes both translators and critics in this absurd story that calls into question the notions of the distinctiveness of original and copy, or of writer and translator. Pierre Menard's task is plainly ridiculous, and the narrator's evaluation of his identical reproduction of Cervantes' novel provides an ironic comment on the pomposity of some critics who presume to judge the quality of translations on idiosyncratic criteria. Nevertheless, despite the comic dimensions of the text, Borges' message is quite serious, and should be heeded by anyone attempting to translate or commenting on anyone else's translation. For exact reproduction is impossible, since the worlds in which the original text and its translation are produced are inevitably different worlds. The task of the translator is therefore to mediate between those two different

---

[1] Jorge Luis Borges, 'Pierre Menard, Author of the *Quixote*', *Labyrinths*, (Harmondsworth: Penguin, 1970), pp. 62–72.

1

moments in time and space, and to produce a text that exists in a relationship with both. It has often been argued that there is no such thing as a 'perfect' translation. Exact reproduction across linguistic boundaries is never possible, and experiments, in which a dozen or more people with similar linguistic competence are asked to translate the same text always result in a range of diverse versions. This diversity reflects the different readings of those individuals, and their different writing styles, for translation always involves that double process of reading and writing. It is important to recognize the inevitability of difference between translations, for all too often translators are accused of betraying the original, of diminishing it or distorting it, as though some perfect single reading might exist and result in a perfect idealized translation. Pierre Menard may be said to have produced just such a perfect version, for his novel does not vary so much as one word from Cervantes' version. That kind of perfection only exists in the realms of absurdist fiction.

Many distinguished translators have explored and sought to elucidate the difference between creating an original text and creating a translation. Boris Pasternak sees the relationship between the original and the translation as 'between what is fundamental and what is derived from it, between a trunk and a cutting'.[2] He states also that the translator must have experienced the impact of the original long before beginning to translate it, so that the eventual product may justly be said to be the fruit and historical consequence of the translator's relationship with the original. This organic image contrasts with the negative rhetoric of accusations of betrayal, and offers an affirmative alternative to the view of translations as a second-rate activity. Before translating Shakespeare, Pasternak acquainted himself with Shakespeare and allowed his potential translations to germinate over several years. Translations, he said,

> are conceivable, because ideally they too should be works of art and, in sharing a common text, should stand on a level with the original through their own uniqueness.[3]

---

[2] Boris Pasternak, 'Notes of a Translator', in Anna Kay France, *Boris Pasternak's Translations of Shakespeare* (Berkeley and Los Angeles: University of California Press, 1978), p. 8.
[3] Ibid. p. 1.

Octavio Paz, similarly, argues that writing and translation are twin processes that are diametrically opposed, since in the former the linguistic sign is fixed in an immutable form whilst in the latter the sign is set free in another language.[4] Both Pasternak's organic growth image of translation and Paz's image of translation as an act of textual liberation present translation in a positive light. In neither of these models is translation seen as a copy of an original, or as a text that somehow has a lower status than that original. Translation is recognized as a creative process, intimately linked to the writing of an original and yet at the same time different, because it necessarily involves reading prior to the writing in the translator's second language.

Often there are idiosyncratic reasons that lead a translator to decide to translate a work. In his preface to his translation of *The Book of the Thousand Nights and A Night*, first published in 1885, Richard Burton explains the factors that led him to undertake the task. The work, he claims, was first of all a labour of love, that sustained him in his periods of depression during what he describes as 'my long years of official exile'.[5] The Jinn, or Genie, of the text carried him back to the 'land of my predilection, Arabia', and the first part of his preface is a lyrical, nostalgic portrait of both the Arabian landscape of his imagination and the people he knew.

But once he had begun his task, he became aware of other translators' attempts at bringing the same text into English. He justifies his own version as being the natural outcome of his life-long interest in Arabian culture, but nevertheless feels he has to compare his work with that of others in order to establish his credibility as a translator. So he argues that Galland's version of 1704 'in no wise represents the eastern original';[6] he claims that other versions are heavily abbreviated and even E.W. Lane is accused of stylistic errors and of being 'at once too Oriental and not Oriental enough'. He reserves higher praise for John Payne's privately printed version, but complains that copies are virtually unobtainable and in any case, Payne did not think to include notes.

Having castigated all fellow translators, Burton explains his own translation strategies. Firstly, he deplores any cuts made to the text, and

[4] Octavio Paz, transl. Irene del Corral, 'Translation: Literature and Letters', in Rainer Schulte and John Biguenet (eds), *Theories of Translation from Dryden to Derrida* (Chicago: University of Chicago Press, 1992), pp. 152–63.
[5] R.F. Burton, *The Book of the Thousand Nights and A Night*, ed. Leonard Smithers (London: H.S. Nichols Ltd, 1897), vol. I, p. xvii.
[6] Ibid. p. xv.

secondly he insists upon the importance of the structure and tone of the original:

> Briefly, the object of this version is to show what 'Thousand Nights and a Night' really is . . . by writing as the Arab would have written in English . . . My work claims to be a faithful copy of the great Eastern saga-book, by preserving intact not only the spirit, but even the *mècanique*, the manner and the matter . . . it retains the scheme of the Nights because they are a prime feature in the original . . .[7]

He takes pains to demonstrate his knowledge of Arabic literary conventions and language registers, pointing out that he has sought to compromise wherever there were dangers such as over-literalness, monotony or strangeness. But on one issue he does not compromise: recognizing that moral conventions vary across cultures, he nevertheless claims that it is his duty to translate the text in its entirety, including even those 'indecencies which can hardly be exaggerated'.[8] Moreover, as he goes on to point out, his own interest in the scabrous has an anthropological dimension. Hence he insists on supplying readers with detailed footnotes, and suggests that any reader who combines his notes with those of E.W. Lane 'will know as much of the Moslem East and more than many Europeans who have spent half their lives in Orient lands'.[9]

It would not be difficult to dismiss Burton as a dirty-minded imperialist who concealed an obsession with pornographic literature beneath a veneer of scholarly concern. This, however, would not be strictly fair, for unlike Lane, who tends to be dismissive of what he perceives as the childlike credulity of orientals (Lane was fond of pointing out that in the Arab world people actually believed the fantastical tales they heard, unlike more 'rational' Europeans) Burton's chief target of attack is his own culture. 'Respectability' is described as a 'whited sepulchre full of uncleanness', whilst 'Propriety' cries out with a 'brazen, blatant voice'.[10] The ultimate aim of Burton's translation, therefore, appears to have been the double one of demonstrating the extent of his encyclopaedic knowledge of Arab culture, for which he had great love and great respect, and attacking the moral conventions of his own culture. There is more vice, he claims, in European novels than in *The Thousand Nights*

---

7 Ibid. pp. xxii–xxiii.
8 Ibid. p. xxv.
9 Ibid. p. xxviii.
10 Ibid. p. xxvii.

and A Night, where there is nothing coarser than may be found in Shakespeare, Rabelais or Swift:

> and at times we descry, through the voluptuous and libertine picture, vistas of a transcendental morality, the morality of Socrates in Plato.[11]

The medieval Arab world is thus compared directly to the ancient Greek world, and both are seen as occupying a higher moral position than contemporary English society. Burton concludes his preface with a bleak statement about the loss of English virtues, and suggests that at the very least his work, and that of other translators, will offer England a means 'of dispelling her ignorance concerning the Eastern races with whom she is continually in contact'.[12]

Of course, reading this preface today, we are aware of the double standard operating behind Burton's declarations of Arabophilia, but then he could not help but be a product of his own age. Hence his translation also mirrors the conventions of his time: the lengthy foot-notes, the use of archaisms, the illustrations and the sheer length of the text, which amounted to sixteen volumes. It is also the case that despite his skill as a reader, despite his linguistic, historical and ethnographical knowledge, Burton did not write very well in English.

If we compare the description of Scheherazade in Burton's version with that of the English rendering of Galland, published as *The Arabian Nights' Entertainments* in one volume in 1843 by William Milner, the differences are immediately apparent:

> Now he (the Grand Wazir) had two daughters, named Shahrazad and Dunyazad, of whom the elder had perused the books, annals and legends of preceding Kings, and the stories, examples and instances of by-gone men and things; indeed it was said that she had collected a thousand books of histories relating to antique races and departed rulers. She had perused the works of the poets and knew them by heart; she had studied philosophy and the sciences, arts and accom-plishment; and she was pleasant and polite, wise, witty, well-read and well-bred.[13]

---

[11] Ibid. p. xxvi.
[12] Ibid. p. xxxii.
[13] Ibid. p. 13.

This is Burton's Scheherazade, an intellectual akin to his own heart, with a pleasant nature and good breeding. He adds a footnote on the orthography of the women's names, noting that Galland had misled him in some unspecified manner. Galland's portrait of Scheherazade is somewhat different:

> The grand vizier . . . had two daughters, the eldest called Scheherazade, and the youngest Dinarzade. The latter was a lady of very great merit, but the elder had courage, wit, and penetration infinitely above her sex. She read much, and had such a prodigious memory that she never forgot any thing she had read. She had successfully applied herself to philosophy, physic, history and the liberal arts; and for verse exceeded the best poets of her time. Besides this, she was a perfect beauty, and all her fine qualifications were crowned by solid virtue.[14]

Clearly this version is highly compressed, but then the publisher states plainly in his preface that he intends to produce the cheapest possible version for English readers, which may also explain why the name of the translator is omitted. However, in this version Scheherazade's intellectual accomplishments are qualified by the reassurance to readers that she was also beautiful and virtuous. Presumably the idea of a woman of such prodigious intellect appealing to the king was so awe-inspiring that some additional attraction needed to be found by the translator to explain all that intelligence away.

But despite the shifts of meaning, which reveal a great deal about the differing ideologies of the translators, there is also a crucial stylistic difference. The Milner version reads like an English novel, at a fast pace, in contemporary English. Burton's text, on the contrary, is weighted down with archaisms and stylistic fussiness. His Scheherazade is alliteratively described as 'wise and witty, well read and well bred', and even in these few lines the verb 'peruse' occurs twice. Despite his prodigious scholarship, Burton's translation was hard to read, and though it sold well, it was the scandalous nature of the content which attracted readers, not the quality of the English. John Addington Symonds, who welcomed the translation, was one of the few critics who did not focus on the content at the expense of discussing the style, and accused Burton of being 'too eager to seize the *mot propre* of his author,

---

14 *The Arabian Nights' Entertainments: consisting of One Thousand and One Stories. In One Volume* (Halifax: William Milner, 1843), p. 8.

or to render that by any equivalent which comes to hand . . . in our vernacular'.[15]

This brief comparison between two versions of the same text exposes the difficulties inherent in evaluating literary translations. If we apply one set of criteria, then Burton's version must rank far above Milner's. It is scrupulous in following the original, it preserves the length and the stylistic shifts, it does not seek to doctor the material to accomodate the tastes of an English readership. In short, it is a translation that is consciously proclaiming itself as a translation. Burton does not seek to acculturate his source text, but rather to take his readers to Arabia. Far from following the example of Pierre Menard, Burton sought to intro-duce material into his own culture that he knew was transgressive, and at the same time he sought to enlighten English readers about Arab culture, hence the orientalizing dimension to his work. In all these respects, Burton's translation deserves praise. The Milner bowdleriza-tion of Galland is a short, populist version that resolutely acculturates both in terms of style and content, to accomodate the demands of the readership in terms of taste. It is easy to read and uncontentious. The preface stresses the pleasurable nature of the stories, and suggests also that since the text is held in the same estimation across Asia as *Don Quixote* is held in Spain, it behoves any 'man of genius and taste' to become acquainted with it before setting off on a visit. Clearly the criteria that led up to the translations were quite different, and are reflected in the finished products. Evaluating them, given such vast differences, is difficult, since the aim of each translator was so utterly different.

Neither translator, however, managed to produce a classic text, that found its way into the English literary system. This is in marked contrast to Edward Fitzgerald's *Rubaiyat of Omar Khayham*, which entered the English system to the point where it came to be regarded as virtually an English poem, or Ezra Pound's Cathay poems, which introduced a fictitious but nonetheless powerfully expressive imaginary China into English. In evaluating the success of a translation, clearly the impact it has is a factor worthy of consideration, and there may be many reasons why neither of these versions of *The Thousand Nights and A Night* (or indeed anyone else's version of the same) ever became fully integrated into English literature. In Burton's case, it may be that despite the initial success in terms of sales, his translation was not very well written and

---

[15] J.S. Symonds, cited in Frank McLynn, *Burton: Snow Upon the Desert* (London: John Murray, 1980), p. 344.

was too close to the stylistic vagaries of the original for it to maintain its status once the scandal surrounding its appearance had died down. Today, we perceive what he produced as a curiosity, and if it is read at all, it is as an orientalist text, not as a work of English literature. For a translation to survive, it has to cross the boundaries between cultures and enter the literature into which it is translated. This can often have a significant impact upon that literature. A great age of literature, Ezra Pound once said, is always a great age of translations.[16] Through translation have frequently come literary innovations. George Puttenham, for example, explains how the sonnet came into English:

> In the latter end of the same king's raigne (Henry VIII) sprong up a new company of courtly makers, of whom *Sir Thomas Wyat* th'elder & *Henry* Earle of Surrey were the two chieftaines, who having travailed into Italie, and there tasted the sweet and stately measures and stile of the Italian poesie as novices newly crept out of the schooles of Dante, Ariosto and Petrarch, they greatly polished our rude and homely manner of vulgar Poesie, from that it had been before . . .[17]

The translators are praised for introducing a new poetic form into English, that has raised the level of native English poetry. Puttenham's view of the benefits of Wyatt and Surrey's translations is unequivocal, and is consistent with the way in which translation was perceived at a time when English literature was in a process of development. Indeed, as recent scholarship in Translation Studies has pointed out, there tends to be a great deal of translation when a literature is developing, whether because that literature perceives itself as marginal or underdeveloped, or because it has reached a plateau and new forms and styles have become necessary for writers to move forward. The European Renaissance was a period of intense translation activity, as was the period in the twelfth and thirteenth centuries when vernacular languages were developing. Later, the Enlightenment was to emerge as a another period of intensive translation, and the great nationalist movements of the nineteenth century in central and southern Europe and in Latin America were also characterized by a great deal of translating.

---

16 Ezra Pound, from 'Elizabethan Classicists', *Egoist* vol. 4, nos. 8–11, vol. 5, no. 1, 1917–18 (reprinted in *Literary Essays* (London: Faber, 1954)).
17 George Puttenham, *The Arte of English Poesie* 1589, book 3, ch. 5, ed. G.D. Willcock and A. Walker (Cambridge: Cambridge University Press, 1936), pp. 148–49.

It also happens that some cultures translate relatively little, and this is currently the case in contemporary Britain. Of course the spread of English as a world language is a factor that cannot be discounted, but nevertheless it is curious that so few publishers should have translation lists, and also that translations should be so unpopular with the majority of readers. Indeed, so reluctant do English readers appear to be to read translations, that frequently texts that are translated are disguised as original works, with the translator's name placed unobtrusively somewhere out of sight or even, as is the case of many translations for the theatre, removed altogether. This English reluctance to accept translations contrasts with the enthusiasm for translations in most other European countries, where flourishing translators' associations enjoy a close relationship with writers' groups and their works reach a large audience.

One explanation for the lack of interest in translation in twentieth-century England, which is in marked contrast with the great interest shown by previous generations, is the shift away from literary cosmopolitanism in the late nineteenth century, towards an increasing political and cultural isolationism. Matthew Arnold may well have pointed out that all literatures are interconnected, Richard Burton may have expressed the hope that his translation would aid international understanding, but in the process of ring-fencing English that took place in the early twentieth century as the subject was seeking to assert itself as a distinct discipline, the links that English literature had always enjoyed with other literatures tended to be downplayed. And, of course, the way in which links across literatures are forged is primarily through translation.

Yet English literature owes great debts to translation. The impact of the Russian and French novel upon the English novel is immense, and all kinds of poetic forms have entered the literature, from the sonnet to the haiku. Strindberg, Ibsen and Chekhov are practically regarded as English playwrights, so often are their plays performed in a variety of different translations and so significant has their influence been. Moreover, a great many texts that are read in translation are simply assumed to have been written in English in the first place. The works of Kant and Schopenhauer, Hegel and Habermass, Foucault and Derrida, countless other philosphers and political scientists are read without regard for their status as translations. The translators of these texts are erased completely; they are virtually invisible.

Invisibility has become a keyword in Translation Studies in the 1990s, as questions are asked about how a translator can be rendered invisible, and why.[18] Clearly, Pasternak, Paz or Pound were very visible indeed, and the habit of translators from non-European languages of including notes to readers also served to emphasize their presence in the text. Pound, however, was continually asserting his rights as a translator, and sniping against what he perceived as negative evaluations of the difficulties of translating. Both Pasternak and Paz write within traditions that respect and admire translation as a highly developed skill, and have consequently had less need to be as defensive.

The process of establishing English as a discipline was accompanied, as many critics have pointed out, by the rediscovery of a specifically English genealogy of texts. Leavis called his a great tradition and set a precedent for the study of the Englishness of English texts that would last for decades. Yet other critics have seen that Englishness very differently. In his brilliant essay, 'Englands of the Mind', Seamus Heaney looks at Ted Hughes, Geoffrey Hill and Philip Larkin and interprets their Englishness as intrinsically connected to other literatures. Hughes, he says, using one of his favoured geological images, 'relies on the nothern deposits, the pagan Anglo-Saxon and Norse elements', while Hill's Anglo-Saxon base is 'modified and amplified by the vocabularies and values of the Mediterranean, by the early medieval Latin influence'. Larkin then,

> completes the picture, because his proper hinterland is the English language Frenchified and turned humanist by the Norman conquest and the Renaissance, made nimble, melodious and plangent by Chaucer and Spenser, and besomed clean of its inkhornisms and its irrational magics by the eighteenth century.[19]

Heaney's own poetry, of course, owes great debts to translation. In this essay, as elsewhere, he shows how literatures are interwoven in such a way that even writers like Hughes, Hill and Larkin, who appear on the surface to empitomize Englishness in their poetry, are nevertheless part of a European literary tradition, in the same way as Byron, Shelley and Keats had been before them. Translation is an unavoidable element

---

18 See: Andre Lefevere, *Translation, Rewriting and the Manipulation of Literary Fame* (London: Routledge, 1993); Susan Bassnett, 'The Visible Translator', *In Other Words* no. 4, Nov. 1994, pp. 11–16; Lawrence Venuti, *The Translator's Invisibility* (London: Routledge, 1995); Ramon Alvarez and Africa Vidal (eds), *Translation, Power, Subversion* (Bath: Multilingual Matters, 1996).

19 Seamus Heaney, 'Englands of the Mind', *Preoccupations: Selected Prose 1968–78* (London: Faber, 1980), p. 151.

of both reading and writing, even if it is not explicitly recognized as such.

What we seem to have in English, then, is a double standard. On the one hand, English literature is steeped in the literature of other cultures and other times, it is intimately inter-related to other literatures and translation has been a prime means of enabling contacts to occur. Yet on the other hand, there is an uneasiness about translation today that is reflected in the low status of translations and the poverty of discussion about translation and its complexities. As Peter Bush succinctly puts it:

> Translation is a continuation of what Jean Genet called the adventure of writing as opposed to the familiar and prosaic bus journey, and it cannot but include subjective, imaginative transformation. It is high time that our attention to (and reviewing of) literary translation moved on from patronizing chatter about deftness, readability or errors; rather, we should focus on the nature and quality of that transformation.[20]

The image of translation as an exciting journey is one that many great translators would doubtless share, and brings us back again to the importance of stressing the creative aspect of translation, rather than perceiving it as some kind of second-rate literary activity. For translation is about wanting to cross boundaries and enter into new territory, whilst the study of translation involves mapping the journeys texts undertake.

The essays collected in this volume look at various aspects of translation, at how translations happen, why they happen and also what happens when translators actually translate. Theo Hermans explores the law of translation in sixteenth-century Europe, examining translation conventions and attitudes to translation that conditioned the ways in which translators worked. This branch of historiographical Translation Studies is gaining ground, for it is through the scrupulous study of contemporary documents on translation that light can be shed on how varied concepts of translation have developed, and how those concepts relate to the actual translations that came into being. As we review the ways in which translation was both described and practised in the past, so we understand more about the processes of literary transfer across cultures.

---

[20] Peter Bush, 'It doesn't sound like English', *TLS* Sept. 6, 1996, p. 11.

In her essay, Felicity Rosslyn contrasts present day assumptions about the 'accuracy' of translation and the demand for 'natural' sounding translations with eighteenth century perceptions, arguing that if we are ever to move across the barrier that separates today's readers from the tradition of using the heroic couplet, we need to look at what translators such as Dryden, Pope or Cowper understood by fidelity. Andre Lefevere, in his essay on the translation of Chinese poetry into English, discusses the way in which translators' strategies can solidify into what he calls a kind of translation poetics, that can restrict the options open to translators and readers. Both Rosslyn and Lefevere are concerned, in different ways, with the problem of how to read translations and how to interpret translation conventions across temporal and cultural gaps.

The question of how translators construct different images of a writer for different audiences at different times is also fundamental to Piotr Kuhiwczak's essay on Slav perceptions of English Romanticism. Translation played a significant role in the development of national literatures across the Slav world in the eighteenth and nineteenth centuries, and the impact of the English (and Scottish) Romantics cannot be underestimated. Kuhiwczak discusses the role of translation in canon formation, pointing out that a very particular notion of Romanticism passed into Polish literature, conditioned more by the needs of the target readership than by the place of certain writers in their own literary system. What Polish literature (and Russian and Czech literatures) needed in the early nineteenth century were texts that could be assimilated into a literature that was developing at the same time as notions of cultural identity were being asserted.

The role of translation in the development of national culture is also the subject of John Corbett's essay, which looks at translation into Scots in the sixteenth and twentieth centuries, the two periods of Scottish literary renaissance. He suggests that there is a separate, distinct tradition of translation into Scots, which has served over the centuries to enrich the literature and enhance the language. This tradition is distinct from the English literary tradition, and is intimately linked to the development of a literature that is identifiably Scottish.

But despite the great cultural forces that propel texts across literatures, there is always a personal dimension. Individuals select texts for translation, and leave their imprint upon those texts. In her essay, Suzanne Stark takes up the more personal aspect of the political implications of translation of George Eliot's translation activity, and argues that through translation Eliot developed not only her style as a writer but also her world view. Translation, Stark believes, thus fulfilled a crucial and indispensible role in George Eliot's progression as a novelist.

There is, as Walter Benjamin famously points out, an idealistic dimension to translation.[21] Translators struggle to recreate a text that already has an existence in another language; always mindful of the constraints that pre-existent text sets down, they nevertheless work to overcome those constraints. Poor Pierre Menard never looked beyond the limits imposed upon him, and in consequence produced only the same text, a stage in what we may assume could be theoretically an endless cycle of sameness. Other translators have been more courageous and more aware of their responsibility not only to the source but also to their eventual readership. For, as Benjamin also reminds us, it is the translator who ultimately assures the survival of the text. By translating, a text reaches a wider pool of readers than the original author can ever have imagined. Borges, the creator of Pierre Menard, knew that only too well: not for nothing is one of his key symbols the library, a world of texts without frontiers.

[21] Walter Benjamin, 'The Task of the Translator', transl. Harry Zohn, in Rainer and Schulte op. cit. pp. 71–83.

The Task of the Translator in the European Renaissance: Explorations in a Discursive Field

THEO HERMANS

THIS IS A PURELY exploratory essay, modest in its aims and scope. It does little more than explore a practical question: whether it is worth investigating in more detail what is best described, in its present state, as a hunch, hardly a hypothesis as yet. The hunch is centred on a word. The exploration circles around it, looking for connections, anchor points, tell-tale signs and traces in the immediate vicinity. It is a compromised search because highly selective. But only a search of this type can, at this stage, produce an answer to the practical question, which is also a question about investment and economy.

The starting point is the word *law*. The law of translation, in the sixteenth century, in Western Europe. Closely connected with it are such terms as the *duty* and the *task* of the translator, terms denoting that which translators commit themselves to when translating, what presents itself to them as obligation and imperative, what they must do to discharge their *office*, their *responsibility* as translators.

The hunch is this: when in the sixteenth-century discourse on translation reference is made to the law of translation or to the translator's duty, task, responsibility or 'office', what is meant is a form of literal or word for word translation. Literalism constitutes the law of translation. Even when it is not expected to be taken in any absolute, 'literal', compelling sense, the notion of literalism as the law remains powerfully present as the ideal of translation, translation's distant but appealing utopia, that which in essence translation ought to be or ought at least to aspire to. Literalism, more than any other form of interlingual processing, embodies the dream of translatability as an exact matching of component parts without loss, excess or deviation. It is a dream at once enticing and exacting, for it demands of the translator ascetic, humbling self-denial. In practice, various more or less pragmatic reasons may induce the individual translator to tone down the ideal or to retreat from it, but they cannot wholly extinguish or remove its appeal. This is not to say that even in theory, literalism reigns supreme. There are those who oppose the notion of literal translation on theoretical as

14

well as on practical grounds. They draw powerful support from the Humanist tradition, and bring rhetorical standards as well as grammatical considerations into play. Their numbers increase especially in the latter half of the sixteenth century. But in the very fact that, more often than not, they too attempt to separate translation from exegesis and consequently feel the need to make taxing demands on the translator, they can be seen to pay indirect homage to literalism as the innermost core and unattainable ideal of translation and as the translator's most fundamental but impossible task. The literalist principle is not fully sidelined until the seventeenth century.

The following paragraphs seek to gather evidence to support this claim. The materials do not consist of actual translations but of statements about translation, since we are looking at the way translation is perceived, conceptualized and theorized. Whether, or to what extent, the theoretical reflections have a bearing on the practice of translation in the period, involves an additional set of issues. They will not be addressed in any detail here. The present essay merely wants to ascertain whether it is at all economical to attempt an interpretation of Renaissance concepts of translation using the notion of literalism as its cornerstone.

Let us take as our starting point two well-known French treatises on poetics from around the mid sixteenth century. They both speak of the 'law' of translation. In Book I, chapter 5, of his *Deffence et illustration de la langue francoyse* (1549) Joachim du Bellay refers to all those admirable gems of eloquence, in prose or verse, which exploit the resources of a particular language in such a way that, he says, their charm and elegance (his term, in French, is 'grace') cannot possibly be rendered by a translator. Add to this the idiomatic differences between languages, Du Bellay continues, and the result is that 'observant la loy de traduyre, qui est n'espacier point hors des limites de l'aucteur, vostre diction sera contrainte, froide, & de mauvaise grace' ['observing the law of translating, which is not to stray beyond the limits set by the author, your diction will be constrained, cold, & lacking in elegance'] (Du Bellay 1948: 36). For this reason translation cannot contribute to linguistic refinement or enrichment, a conclusion Du Bellay draws, explicitly and aggressively, at the end of the next chapter.[1]

---

[1] 'Mais que diray-je d'aucuns, vrayement mieux dignes d'estre appelés traditeurs que traducteurs? veu qu'ilz trahissent ceux qu'ilz entreprennent exposer (. . .) et encore se prennent aux poëtes, genre d'aucteurs certes auquel, si je scavoy' ou vouloy' traduyre, je m'adroisseroy' aussi peu, à cause de ceste

But what does Du Bellay mean when he speaks of 'the law of translating'? The spatial imagery in the wording ('espacier', 'limites') leaves room for speculation regarding the precise extent of the translator's leeway, but it is clear that 'the law of translating' implies confinement to a narrowly circumscribed area, so much so that it produces aesthetically unacceptable results. This is spelled out in the letter to Jean de Morel with which some years later Du Bellay prefaces his French version (for despite his strictures Du Bellay, as we know, does translate) of the fourth book of Virgil's *Aeneid*. Appealing to 'ceux qui entendent & la peine & les lois de traduire' ['those who understand both the labour and the laws of translating'], he points out the utter impossibility of conveying even the original author's shadow if the translator is held to render everywhere 'përiode pour përiode, epithete pour epithete, nom propre pour nom propre, & finablement dire ny plus ny moins, & non autrement' ['period for period, epithet for epithet, proper noun for proper noun, and finally saying neither more nor less, nor anything different']; for this reason he feels he has honourably acquitted himself of his task ('son devoir') by translating in a freer, more compensatory vein (Du Bellay 1931, VI: 249–50). The law of translating is evidently quite strict, and does not allow the translator to stray far from the words of the original.

Both the way Du Bellay here fills in the notion of the 'law' of translation and the terms he used in the earlier *Deffence et illustration* to describe the unattractive effect of translations carried out according to this 'law' – a diction deprived of eloquence and hence 'constrained, cold, & lacking in elegance' – resemble those employed elsewhere, by other writers in discussions unequivocally aimed at literal or word for word translation.

A case in point would be chapter 6, 'Des traductions', of Jacques Peletier du Mans' *Art poétique* of 1555 (Peletier 1990: 262–65). Here Peletier considers both the effects of literal translation and its utopia. Having explained – in marked contrast to Du Bellay – that the translator subjects himself ('s'asservit') not only to the *inventio* and the *dispositio* but as far as possible also to the *elocutio* of his author and that

divinité d'invention qu'ilz ont plus que les autres, de ceste grandeur de style, magnificence de motz, gravité de sentences, audace & variété de figures, & mil' autres lumieres de poësie: bref ceste energie, & ne scay quel esprit, qui est en leurs ecriz, que les Latins appelleroient *genius*. Toutes les quelles choses se peuvent autant exprimer en traduisant, comme un peintre peut representer l'ame avecques le cors de celuy qu'il entreprent tyrer apres le naturel.' (Du Bellay 1948, Chap. VI).

in so doing he rightfully earns for translation a place in the world of art ('aient donc les Traductions place en notre Art, puisque'elles se font par art'), he goes on to state that its 'law' however is understood by few ('. . . que la loi en est entendue de peu de gens'). Peletier illustrates his point by offering a correct reading of the famous but frequently misinterpreted *fidus interpres* passage in Horace's Art of Poetry, i.e. a reading that has Horace indeed affirming that the faithful translator translates word for word ('Et ne me peux assez ébahir de ceux, qui pour blâmer la traduction de mot à mot, se veulent aider de l'autorité d'Horace, quand il dit: *Nec verbum verbo curabis reddere, fidus Interpres*: là où certes Horace parle tout au contraire de leur intention', Peletier 1990: 264). Following an aside on the metre in Virgil's third Eclogue he returns to his main point and rounds off the chapter. The concluding passage is worth quoting in full:

> Suivant notre propos, les Traductions de mot à mot n'ont pas grâce: non qu'elles soient contre la loi de Traduction: mais seulement pour raison que deux langues ne sont jamais uniformes en phrases. Les conceptions sont communes aux entendements de tous hommes: mais les mots et manières de parler sont particuliers aux nations. Et qu'on ne me vienne point alléguer Cicéron: lequel ne loue pas le Traducteur consciencieux. Car aussi ne fais-je. Et ne l'entends point autrement, sinon que le Translateur doive garder la propriété et le naïf de la Langue en laquelle il translate. Mais certes je dis qu'en ce que les deux Langues symboliseront: il ne doit rien perdre des locutions, ni même de la privauté des mots de l'Auteur, duquel l'esprit et la subtilité souvent consiste en cela. Et qui pourrait traduire tout Virgile en vers français, phrase pour phrase, et mot pour mot: ce serait une louange inestimable. Car un Traducteur, comment saurait-il mieux faire son devoir, sinon en approchant toujours le plus près qu'il serait possible de l'Auteur auquel il est sujet? Puis, pensez quelle grandeur ce serait de voir une seconde Langue répondre à toute l'élégance de la première: et encore avoir la sienne propre. Mais, comme j'ai dit, il ne se peut faire. (Peletier 1990: 265)

> [To continue, word for word Translations are unshapely. This is not because they are incompatible with the law of Translation, but merely because no two languages are the same in their expression. Concepts are common to the understanding of all, but each nation has its own words and manners of speaking. And let no-one invoke Cicero here, who does not praise the conscientious Translator. Indeed neither do I. All I mean is that the Translator should respect the propriety and idiom of the Language into which he translates.

But I do say that as regards that which the two Languages express, the Translator should lose nothing of the way of speaking or even of the idiosyncratic usage of the Author, whose wit and subtlety often consist in this. And if someone were able to translate Virgil into French verse, sentence for sentence, and word for word: what glorious praise that would bring. For how could a Translator discharge his duty better, if not by sticking as closely as possible to the Author to whom he has subjected himself? And imagine how splendid it would be to see one Language echo all the elegance of the other, and still retain its own. But, as I said, that is impossible.]

Peletier's comment on the ungainly nature of literal translations obviously recalls Du Bellay's censure ('. . . de mauvaise grace', '. . . n'ont pas grâce'). More striking however are the ambivalences in Peletier's words. Literal translations, for him, are not in conflict with the law of translation, which suggests that the law itself is something else. But what exactly? And where does the compatibility between the law and literal translation begin and end? At first it looks as if Peletier puts some distance between literalism and the law of translation, hence the concessionary 'non qu'elles soient contre la loi de Traduction'. Like Cicero, he declines to praise the 'conscientious' literalist translator. Later in the passage it appears however that it is only in operating as literally as possible, in rendering Virgil 'phrase pour phrase, et mot pour mot', in reducing the distance separating translator and author to the absolute minimum ('en approchant toujours le plus près qu'il serait possible de l'Auteur auquel il est sujet'), that the translator can hope fully to acquit himself of his task ('son devoir'). Such a translator would then deserve all due praise and fame ('louange', 'grandeur'). But how much is that, and what does the translator's 'devoir' consist in?

Earlier in the chapter Peletier had emphasized that translations are generally held in lower esteem than original writings. Having characterized translation as 'une besogne de plus grand travail que de louange', he observed that even if the translator works 'well and faithfully' ('si vous rendez bien en fidèlement') it is invariably the original which receives all the praise ('le plus de l'honneur en demeure à l'original'), and however good the rendering, the difference in status between translator and original author always remains ('Somme, un Traducteur n'a jamais le nom d'Auteur'). At the same time Peletier had asserted, paradoxically, that 'a good translation is more valuable than a poor original' ('une bonne Traduction vaut trop mieux qu'une mauvaise invention'). He resolves the paradox with a reference to the perceived status of translators and original writers ('authors'): a good translation may be more valuable than a poor specimen of *inventio*, but the translator will lose out either way. If he elects to render a poor original he will be blamed for having made the wrong choice, and if he provides a good rendering of a worthy original it is that original's author who collects the prize. This perception only changes when translators are also themselves authors of original works, as Peletier explains in connection with the use of neologisms. As regards neologisms he recommends great caution on the translator's part, precisely because readers have a different perception of translated and original writings: 'Un Traducteur, s'il n'a fait voir ailleurs quelque chose du sien, n'a pas cette faveur des Lecteurs en cas de mots, combien que soit celui qui plus en a affaire. Et pour cela est moins estimé l'office de traduire' ['A Translator who has not published work of his own elsewhere, cannot count on the Readers' indulgence with respect to words, even though he is most concerned with them. This is why the profession of translating is less esteemed.']. Boldness or inventiveness are not readily associated with the translator's job. Even in translating an outstanding author the translator should resort to 'new' words only when there are absolutely no others available and when the persistent use of periphrasis and circumlocution would produce too great a 'déplaisir' in the reading.

While the praise and fame a translator can hope for in Peletier's terms thus remain a rather paradoxical point, it is clearly tied to the difference in status accorded to translator and author. It is also the difference in perceived status between translators and authors which puts the former in their place and restricts their room for manoeuvre. The more they are seen as translators and present themselves as translators, the more narrowly circumscribed their space becomes. Leaving aside those literary devices that lend a text its 'grâce', it would seem that the core requirement is for the translator to render 'phrase pour phrase, et mot pour mot', effectively closing the gap between himself and his author. Such translations however are not really acceptable to the aesthetically sensitive reader. They can be squared with the law of translation, but not with artistic expression. This appears to be the rub in Peletier's chapter. If translation is to have a place in handbooks on the art of poetry, then it ought to do the impossible. It ought to reduce to nil the distance between original and translation by clinging to the former's every word and nuance, and simultaneously to retain the stylistic refinement of the donor text while respecting the integrity of the receptor language. This, Peletier realizes, is asking too much ('Mais, comme j'ai dit, il ne se peut faire'). Translation cannot reach beyond itself. The fact that different languages possess different grammatical and idiomatic structures and hence different rhetorical resources renders total correspondence utopian. Yet total correspondence, the absence of distance, is what the duty of the translator and the law of translation demand.

Faced with this dilemma, Peletier ends his chapter by registering the impasse it leads into, yet without proposing a way out. Du Bellay, as we saw, solved the problem by dismissing translation as an instrument of artistic expression. In fact, whenever 'eloquence' was involved he emphatically preferred imitation to translation. Peletier leaves the impasse unresolved, and this also allows him to leave the duty of the translator and the law of translation unchallenged. Translation is still strictly circumscribed: translation in the strict sense means a strict form of translating. Deviation, allowing space between donor and receptor text, compromises the integrity of the translation and, by implication, of the translator. It cannot be reconciled with the requirement of loyal and 'conscientious' faithfulness and lays the translator open to the charge of betrayal and fraud. When he fails to pay proper attention to 'la propriété des mots et locutions' the translator 'défraude le sens de l'Auteur'.

The legal and moral overtones in the notions of fidelity and fraud, the translator's professional duty and translation's law, all echo Saint Jerome's famous Letter to Pammachius of ca. 395 (Letter 57), also known as De optimo genere interpretandi (Jerome 1953). That document is directly relevant here. It too speaks of the translator's duty, and of literal translation. It also links the two concepts, be it – as in Peletier's chapter – in a less than straightforward manner. Let us have a closer look. As is well known, Jerome's Letter was written in self-defence. The immediate cause was a public and potentially damaging attack, which Jerome puts before Pammachius in the opening paragraphs. There he explains that shortly before he had, in response to an urgent request and from a friend working at great speed, made a Latin translation of a Greek text, which he had further elucidated and annotated in the margin. Although the translation had been intended for strictly private use, it ended up in the wrong hands, and Jerome stood accused of unprofessional conduct. The accusation levelled against him, he says, boiled down to either professional incompetence, in that he did not know how to translate, or criminal bad faith, in that he had refused to translate properly ('. . . aut nescui . . . interpretari, aut nolui . . . alterum error . . . alterum crimen'). Either way he was charged with having delivered a fraudulent product in that he had not translated word for word ('. . . contionentur me falsarium, me verbum non expressisse de verbo'). What was expected of a translator, clearly (or: as Jerome makes it appear), was just such a translation, a word for word rendering. The fact that Jerome's failure to produce such a version could become the cause for a public attack against him suggests that the word for word rule, as a normative expectation, was strong and widely accepted.

In the course of his defence Jerome never challenges the validity of the rule as such. The nearest he comes to it is when, speaking for the more cultured readers ('eruditi'), he sneers at the claim to truth and integrity, the supposed 'veritas interpretationis' of the literalists. His tactic, rather, is to proclaim an alternative mode, that of translating 'ad sensum', which he claims is applicable to all types of texts with the exception of Scripture, and which separates the cultured, discerning translators from the mass of diligent but dull literalists. His declaration is famous enough: 'Ego enim non solum fateor, sed libera voce profiteor me in interpretatione Graecorum absque scripturis sanctis, ubi et verborum ordo mysterium est, non verbum e verbo sed sensum exprimere de sensu' ['I not only declare but loudly proclaim that in translating from the Greek, except for the sacred scriptures where even the order of the words is a mystery, I translate not word for word but sense for sense.'] (Jerome 1953: 59). But even after his persuasive argumentation regarding the near-impossibility of avoiding either omissions or additions when attempting to translate stylistically sophisticated source texts, Jerome still works a peculiar paradox into his key statement of the translator's dilemma which follows a little later: 'si ad verbum interpretor, absurde resonant; si ob necessitatem aliquid in ordine, in sermone mutavero, ab interpretis videbor officio recessisse' ['if I translate word for word, the result sounds absurd; if of necessity I change anything in the order or the manner of speaking, I will seem to have fallen short of the duty of a translator'] (Jerome 1953: 61).[2] It is Jerome's reference to 'the duty of a translator' ('interpretis officium') which recalls Peletier's 'l'office de traduire' and the 'devoir' of the translator. Jerome's dilemma too is like Peletier's. As Jerome puts it, literal translation produces unacceptable results which grate on the ear, but moving away from it means incurring censure of a different kind, as it amounts to abandoning one's post, failing to live up to one's responsibility, defaulting on one's obligation – on that which is precisely

---

[2] Jerome is here actually quoting from his own preface to his translation of the *Chronicles* of Eusebius, which dates from *ca.* 381.

what the translator should be doing. In arguing against literal translation, Jerome at the same time confirms the general validity of the rule.

Immediately after he has proclaimed his own policy of translating 'ad
sensum' rather than 'ad verbum', Jerome invokes the authority of
Cicero, from whose *De optimo genere oratorum* he goes on to quote. Here
again something odd happens. The passage Jerome selects is the one
where Cicero explains that in rendering the two Greek orations before
him he did not count out the words individually as coins but paid the
whole amount at once. Surprisingly, perhaps, Jerome also repeats as part
of his quotation Cicero's remark that in so doing he was aware that he
was not operating in the manner of a translator but in that of an orator
('nec converti ut interpres, sed ut orator') – the implication of which
must be, even though Jerome obviously does not draw attention to it,
that in Cicero's view going about translating in the manner of a
translator ('ut interpres') does mean counting out the words individually as coins, i.e. translating word for word. The reason why Cicero
prefers to work 'ut orator' rather than 'ut interpres' in the versions of
Aeschines and Demosthenes to which *De optimo genere oratorum* serves
as a preface, is that he is intent not on reproducing in Latin what the
Greek orators actually said, but on creating a Latin model of the Attic
style of oratory which will be able to displace the Greek sources
(Copeland 1991: 45ff).

A very similar duality appears in the opening paragraphs of Cicero's
De finibus, which Jerome does not mention but which tie in with the
comments in *De optimo genere* and additionally throw up a reference to
the 'task' of the translator. *De finibus*, like *De optimo genere*, arises out
of the desire to appropriate Greek sources in such a way as to render
them redundant. Early on in this work Cicero voices his disapproval of
those Roman Graecophiles who look down on their own Latin culture
but delight in literal translations from the Greek ('ad verbum e Graecis
expressas'). He goes on to state that he could of course have translated
in the same plain manner ('si plane sic verterem') but decided on this
occasion to do more, to go beyond what is expected of translators or
what is regarded as part of the translators' task ('interpretum munus').
The result of this deliberate choice is a type of rendering comparable
to that used in connection with the Greek orations, but now applied
to the domain of philosophy and ethics. Of interest in the present
context is the fact that when, both in *De optimo genere* and in *De finibus*,
Cicero speaks of 'translating' he employs the same verbs ('vertere',
'convertere') but suggests that the activity they refer to can be performed in two markedly different ways, one of them 'as a translator' ('ut

interpres'), the other 'as an orator' ('ut orator') or in the similar but unnamed capacity applicable to the discursive subject of *De finibus*. The manner which he calls 'plain' because it is unadorned, which does not enjoy the cultural prestige of the 'ut orator' style, and which humbly but dutifully counts out the words one by one, is the manner 'ut interpres', the manner associated with the task or duty ('munus') of the translator.[3]

The question of whether, or to what extent, Jerome deliberately reduced the complexity of Cicero's pronouncements and twisted their intent to serve the purposes of his own polemic against his anonymous detractors, need not detain us here. The relevant point is that explicitly in Cicero and somewhat more implicitly in Jerome we encounter the notion of word for word translation as most closely associated with, as actually constituting the proper task and duty ('officium', 'munus') of the translator, and of the plainly honest, faithful, loyal and therefore reliable translator in particular. That does not mean that detailing the duty of the translator in individual cases is straightforward or uncontroversial. On the contrary, the alternative 'ad sensum' mode will be a constant presence and it has cultural prestige and self-confidence on its side. But it does mean that when the proponents of the more liberal line criticize the literal tendency on the grounds that its word for word method results in texts so clumsy as to be unfit for circulation in cultured society, the defence of the strict 'ad verbum' manner rests pre-eminently on moral considerations of trustworthiness, integrity, reliability and incorruptibility.

In the early Middle Ages, when the Christian mistrust of Classical rhetoric acts as a powerful spur, this line of argument in support of literalism is eagerly taken up. When Saint Augustine, in *On Christian Doctrine*, becomes aware of the potentially damaging differences between existing Latin versions of Scripture, he recommends using the most literal translations, as these must be deemed least likely to engender corrupt readings. The word for word manner which Jerome reserved as appropriate only for the Bible is subsequently adopted for other discourses as well. Boethius puts the case very forcefully, and others follow suit.[4] Being good Christians, they happily accept the taint of being no more than faithful translators ('fidi interpretis culpa') if that allows them to lay claim to total integrity and access to the naked truth,

---

[3] For more detailed discussions, see Hoskin 1985 and Copeland 1991, Chapters 1 and 2.

[4] See Schwarz 1985: 43–48; Copeland 1991: 52–55.

stripped of all rhetorical embellishment and corruption, just as the Biblical word itself is both plain and true. As Boethius puts it in the early sixth century, in connection with Porphyry's *Isagoge*: 'in these writings in which knowledge of the matter is sought' ('in his scriptis in quibus rerum cognitio quaeritur'), what matters is 'not the charm of a sparkling style, but the uncorrupted truth' ('non luculentae orationis lepos, sed incorrupta veritas'), and this is achieved 'through sound and irreproachable translation' ('per integerrimae translationis sinceritatem'; Copeland 1991: 52; Schwarz 1945: 43–48).

The marked emphasis on purity and integrity ('incorrupta veritas', 'integerrimae translationis sinceritas') leads into paradoxes. On the one hand, because of the narrow limits which this mode of translating chooses to impose on itself, the end product clearly advertizes its status as a translated text through its forced, tormented expression – in which it takes a martyr-like, anti-rhetorical pride because it is precisely the textual ungainliness of the product which signals its integrity as a translation. The translator himself, on the other hand, does everything in his power to expunge his presence and erase his intervention by ensuring that every word of the donor text is covered so scrupulously that its integrity is never compromised. The ascetic self-restraint demanded by literalism seeks to ensure above all that the transfer from one language to another will be so close, so word for word, as to allow no slippage, no hairline crack through which meaning might ooze out or rhetorical or interpretive corruption seep in. But the double movement, in which the translated text vaunts its translated status through its deliberate hideousness and the translator does his utmost to disappear as an actively interpreting and meaning-producing subject, also guarantees that the translator has not wrongfully appropriated anything that is not his, and simultaneously – another aspect of the same issue – that he cannot be held responsible for merely handing on someone else's statements. The intermediary does not intervene in any substantive way. The ironic pride of the absent, empty-handed translator consists in the awareness, or at any rate in the ideological self-assurance, of offering the reader an absolutely clear view of the original.

Considerations like these appear to mark the dividing line between the translator on one side and, on the other, the exegete, as the provider of paraphrases, glosses, commentaries and interpretations. When, in the early medieval period, John Scotus Eriugena is criticized for the obscurity of one of his translations, he counters with the observation that he was only the work's translator, not its expositor ('videat me interpretem huius operis esse, non expositorem', Copeland 1991: 52,

91) – and it is an appeal to the notion of the 'faithful translator' ('fidus interpres') which allows him to establish the opposition. It is precisely in terms of oppositions like these that in the early Renaissance the 'office' of the translator and the domain of translation in the 'strict' sense will be determined. At the end of the fourteenth century the Greek scholar Manuel Chrysoloras, who had left Byzantium a few years earlier and settled in Florence, was recorded as disapproving of word for word 'conversio', because it could easily pervert the thought expressed in the source text, but remarked in the same breath that departing from the words of the original and from the 'propriety' of the Greek amounted to abandoning the 'office' of translator for that of exegete ('eum non interpretis, sed exponentis officio uti'; Norton 1984: 35).

Around the mid-fifteenth century the Spanish Humanist Alfonso de Madrigal, translating the Chronici canones of Eusebius into Spanish and writing a Latin commentary on them (not printed until the early years of the sixteenth century), speaks in similar terms of two modes of translation, one of which however he describes as extending beyond translation. The first, word for word, is called 'interpretacion o translacion'. The other, which does not follow the words, he calls 'exposicion o comento o glosa', and this form, he says, frequently requires many additions and changes ('muchas adiciones et mudamientos'), so that in the end the work is no longer the original author's but the expositor's ('por lo cual non es obra del autor, mas del glosador', Keightley 1977: 246).[5] But additions and changes are irreconcilable with the 'duty' of the translator, as Madrigal indicates in his Latin commentary on Eusebius, with an unmistakable nod in Jerome's direction: when the translator 'changes something in the order of words or the manner of speaking, he can do so in two ways, both of which lead away from the translator's duty: by adding something, or by changing as well as adding, and then he writes commentaries rather than a

---

[5] The quotation is as follows: 'Dos son las maneras de trasladar: una es de palabra a palabra, et llamase interpretacion; otra es poniendo la sentencia sin seguir las palabras, la qual se faze comunmente por mas luengas palabras, et esta se llama exposicion o comento o glosa. La primera es de mas autoridad, la segunda es mas clara para los menores ingenios. Enla primera non se añade, et porende sienpre es de aquel que la primero fabrico. Enla segunda se fazen muchas adiciones et mudamientos, por lo qual non es obra des autor, mas del glosador.' The opening rubric of the translation reads: 'Aqui comiença la interpretacion o translacion del libro Delas cronicas o tiempos de Eusebio cesariensse, de latin en fabla castellana' (Keightly 1977: 246, 244).

translation, so that the original work does not remain intact but a new work comes into being which is a commentary or exposition of the first one' ('qui mutat in ordine vel in sermone, dupliciter potest mutare, et utroque modo ab interpretis recidit officio; primo modo addendo aliud, vel mutando ordinem cum aliquali tamen additione, et tunc comentarios agit, non translationem, et iam non videtur manere opus principale, sed aliud novum opus conditur, quod prioris comentum vel expositio est'; Keightley 1977: 246). True to this principle Madrigal declares his intention to keep his translation of Eusebius separate from his commentary on this author, adding that it is translating which is the more difficult task since it has to be done word for word in the interest of the original's integrity, even if this runs the risk of producing obscure and therefore demanding passages (ibid.: 244–45).[6]

With Madrigal we have returned to the Renaissance. In sixteenth-century pronouncements on translation the term 'officium' or a modern vernacular variant occurs a number of times, usually with reference to the task, responsibility, obligation or duty of *the* translator in a general or generic sense. Often it is flanked by the demand or the wish to translate literally or as literally as possible. This striving is seen as the pre-eminent quality of the 'faithful' translator, who discharges his 'officium' by translating in a manner characterized as 'faithful', 'loyal', 'truthful', 'conscientious', 'scrupulous', 'religious' or a similar adjective. The adjectives in turn appear to offer word for word translators moral compensation for the discomfort they find themselves in, since their sense of duty puts them in a position they describe as constrained, unfree, enthralled, narrowly hemmed in, bound hand and foot. If their service and sacrifice consist in this, it also grants them a degree of safety which the paraphrast has to do without. Since paraphrase, glossing and explication inevitably mean the use of words which are the commentator's own, they increase the risk of error, misinterpretation, misrepresentation and corruption.

As for the term 'officium' itself, and its association with the principle of translating word for word: Erasmus uses it in a letter of 1506, which will be discussed below. In 1543 the Swiss humanist Henricus Glareanus demonstrates that contrary to prevailing opinion the famous 'fidus interpres' passage in Horace's *Art of Poetry* does in fact identify the 'verbum verbo' manner of translating as constituting the translator's 'officium' (Norton 1984: 83) – a few years later Peletier du Mans will

---

6   See also Norton 1984: 31–32 and Santoyo 1987: 36.

follow Glareanus's reading of the passage, as we saw. Even at the very end of the sixteenth century editions of Horace's poetry appeared which had in the margin, next to the 'fidus interpres' lines, the gloss 'interpretis officium' (e.g. Horatius 1594: 150). In the preface to his Spanish version of the Song of Songs, around 1561, Luis de León discusses the translator's 'oficio' in terms of literal translation; more about this below too. When in 1566 the Flemish translator Marcus Antonius Gillis publishes a Dutch version of the emblems of the Hungarian humanist Johannes Sambucus, he declares to have acquitted himself of 'the office of a faithful Translator' ('d'officie eens ghetrouwen Oversetters') by translating Sambucus's very compact Latin word for word (Hermans 1996: 56). In 1595 Blaise de Vigenère points out that in his rendering of Tasso he has deviated from what he calls, ironically this time, the correct way to translate, which is 'toute à la lettre, ainsi qu'on est obligé es traduction' (Horguelin 1981: 69). Around 1603 the Spanish translator Gregorio Morillo speaks of both the 'office' and the 'laws' which define the faithful translator's activity ('officio', 'las leyes del intérprete fiel'; Santoyo 1987: 73–74). When the Antwerp Jesuit Andreas Schottus offers a typology of different forms of translation in his book on Ciceronian imitation (1610), he also picks up the Ciceronian term 'munus interpretis' and associates it with literalism (Rener 1989: 287).

Schottus' chapter on translation ('Liber IV: De optimo genere interpretandi Ciceronem', Schottus 1610: 268ff.) is in fact a late but powerful assertion of the literalist principle. He begins by distinguishing two kinds of 'interpretatio', one called 'metaphrase', the other 'paraphrase'. Paraphrase, which he considers to be a matter of amplification, explanation and commentary, has three subdivisions: 'historica', 'critica' or 'narrativa', and the more flowery 'artificiosa'. Metaphrase, which he regards as translation proper, comes in two kinds: 'faithful' or 'scrupulous' ('religiosa'), and 'arbitrary'. Related to the 'faithful' mode but less strict is an intermediate 'freer' kind ('liberior'), which operates on a sense-for-sense principle and is the one Cicero claimed for himself as a more learned mode. Yet Schottus uses quotations from Cicero's own works to interrogate his subject on the vexed question of what exactly constitutes the translator's 'officium' or 'munus' ('Quodnam, Marce Tulli, munus Interpretis?', 1610: 321), and concludes it can only be a literalist 'ad verbum' mode. Horace is then brought in to support this view. The way in which Schottus describes literalism has a familiar ring by now. The 'Fidus Interpres' is characterized as one who 'renders word for word in such a way that he does not stray a fingernail's breadth from the author he has undertaken to translate' ('qui ad verbum sic reddit, ut ne latum quidem unguem ab auctore, quem interpretandum suscepit, discedat', 1610: 318), and who is so well versed in both languages that he is able to convey the original author's sense properly and lucidly ('sit modo linguae utriusque ex aequo peritus, ut sensa auctoris Latine ac perspicue convertat'). Whereas the 'freer' mode is content, in the manner of the orators, to represent the overall sense or meaning or idea rather than counting out the individual words ('Affinis huic, sed largior, quem *liberiorem* nomino, qui non tam adnumerat verba, quam appendit, Oratorum more, sententiam integre repraesentasse contentus', and 'Hanc interpretationem liberam κατα γνώμων, φράσιν ἡ διάνοιαν vocaverim, quae scriptoris sententiam incolumem magis quam verba conservat', 1610: 318, 319), the word for word method is also called – with a reference to the Roman Emperor Justinian – the 'step-for-step' method because it traces its model's every footstep and counts its every word ('Fidelis autem versio est, κατα λέξιν; quam κατα πόδα vocari a Graecis auctor est Iustinianus Imp. L. I. D. *De Jure enucleando*: cum Interpretes iisdem quasi vestigiis sic inhaerent, ut verba verbis quasi dimensa ac paria reddant', 1610: 319). This is reinforced once more when Schottus sums up the Ciceronian and Horatian view of the task of the faithful translator as consisting in 'rendering into another language, in good faith, word for word, adding nothing, omitting nothing, changing nothing' ('Quodnam, Marce Tulli, *munus Interpretis*? nonne ad verbum, fide bona, in aliam transfundere linguam, nihil ut de tuo addes, demas nihil, nihil denique immutes'). For Schottus, clearly, the core of the concept of translation lies here. It is essentially a matter of counting words in a state of absolute loyalty and self-negation, in contrast with the sense-for-sense mode of the freer translators and, beyond that, with both the wilful appropriation of the 'arbitrary' mode and the expansiveness of paraphrase.

Schottus' book already takes us into the seventeenth century. By then the objections against the literalist principle have become loud and numerous. Of course, the objections were always there, from Saint Jerome onwards. In the Renaissance they will be heard increasingly strongly, coming primarily from Humanist translators and from those vernacular translators who take their cue from the Humanist tradition. When Jacques Amyot, for example, writes the preface to his celebrated *Lives* of Plutarch (1559) he does not even mention the word for word manner in his description of the translator's 'office':

... je prie les lecteurs de vouloir considerer que l'office d'un propre traducteur ne gist pas seulement à rendre fidèlement la sentence de son autheur, mais aussi à représenter aucunement et à adombrer la forme du style et manière de parler d'iceluy (Horguelin 1981: 66)

[I ask the readers to consider that the office of a proper translator does not consist only in faithfully rendering his author's meaning but also in somehow representing and adumbrating his style and manner of speaking]

These principles will become predominant in the seventeenth century. But let us return first to the sixteenth, to Erasmus and Luis de León.

As early as 1503, in a letter concerning his first translation, three orations by Libanius of Antiochia rendered from Greek into Latin, Erasmus shows his familiarity with Cicero's statement, in *De optimo genere*, about translating as settling an account at once instead of counting out the words one by one like individual coins. He immediately adds, however, that as a novice translator ('novus interpres') he has preferred to be too scrupulous ('religiosus') rather than too bold ('religiosior esse malui quam audacior', 17 November 1503; Allan 1906, no. 177). His letter of 24 January 1506, where he discusses his translation of the *Hecuba* of Euripides, takes up the same idea. Here Erasmus says he has chosen not to avail himself of the liberty which Cicero grants the translator and that, still regarding himself as a 'novus interpres', he has again preferred to err on the side of scruple, even of superstition, rather than of licentiousness ('ut superstitiosior viderer alicui potius quam licentior'; Allan 1906, no. 188). As regards the 'office' of the translator he is dismissive both of the paraphrastic alternative, as a flight into ineptitude, like a squid enveloping itself in a dark cloud, and of the expansive rhetorical option, as being an unwarranted, self-indulgent addition.[7]

---

[7] The relevant passage reads as follows: '. . . dum versum versui, dum verbum pene verbo reddere nitor, dum ubique sententiae vim ac pondus summa cum fide Latinis auribus appendere studeo: sive quod mihi non perinde probatur illa in vertendis authoribus libertas, quam Marcus Tullius ut aliis permittit, ita ipse (pene dixerim immodice) usurpavit; sive quod novus interpres in hanc malui peccare partem, ut superstitiosior viderer alicui potius quam licentior, id est ut littoralibus in harenis nonnunquam haerere viderer potius quam fracta nave mediis natare fluctibus; maluique committere ut eruditi candorem et concinnitatem carminis in me forsitan desyderarent quam fidem. Denique nolui paraphrasten professus eam mihi latebram parare qua multi suam palliant inscitiam, ac loliginis in morem, ne depraehendantur, suis se tenebris involuunt. Iam vero quod Latinae tragoediae grandiloquentiam, ampullas et sesquipedalia, ut Flaccus ait, verba hic nusquam audient, mihi non debent

Both letters are written by a translator who emphatically acknowledges his own inexperience; and the second letter cannot be said to
advocate the word for word mode in any exclusive sense, since he has
also endeavoured to cover 'the power and weight of the thought with
the utmost faithfulness' ('sententiae vim ac pondus summa cum fide').
Their interest lies in the fact that they associate faithfulness with the
move closer to the words, and, as in the case of Alfonso de Madrigal
half a century earlier, distrust the translator's own interpretive additions. In so doing they mark the dividing line between the 'proper'
translator on the one hand and the paraphrastic and rhetorical translator on the other. It is this distinction which is drawn also, and more
sharply, by Luis de León, in the prologue to his translation of the Song
of Songs (*Traduccion literal y declaración del libro de los Cantares de
Salomón*, ca. 1561; Santoyo 1987: 65–66; López García 1996: 77–79).
For Luis, the task of the translator is quite different from that of the
commentator ('entiendo sea diferente el oficio del que traslada . . . del
que las explica y declara'). The commentator should copiously explain
the sense and substance of the text before him, in his own words ('El
extenderse diciendo, y el declarar copiosamente la razon que se en-
tienda . . . eso quédese para el que declara, cuyo oficio es'). The
translator's task, by contrast, consists in counting out the words exactly
if that were possible, providing for each word another one possessing
the same weight, value and range of meanings ('el que traslada ha de
ser fiel y cabal, y si fuere posible, contar las palabras, para dar otras
tantas, y no más, de la misma manera, cualidad, y condición y variedad
de significaciones que las originales tienen'). Like Peletier du Mans,
who, as we saw, would have preferred to see all of Virgil translated into
French in this manner but realized it could not be done, so Luis de León
too has to admit in the end that due to the structural asymmetry
between languages a strict word for word rendering is impracticable and
he has been obliged to intervene to some extent, in the interest of
intelligibility ('Bien es verdad que, trasladando el texto, no pudimos
tan puntualmente ir con el original, y la cualidad de la sentencia y
propiedad de nuestra lengua nos forzó á que añadiésemos alguna
palabrilla, que sin ella quedaría oscurísimo el sentido; pero estas son
pocas').
Despite this pragmatic retreat, which Luis does his best to belittle

imputare, si interpretis officio fungens eius quem verti pressam sanitatem
elegantiamque referre malui quam alienum tumorem, qui me nec alias mag-
nopere delectat (Allan 1906: 419–20).

(he says he only added a few little words, 'alguna palabrilla', and 'estas son pocas'), the prologue is significant for the way it posits literalism as the ideal form of translation and directly associates the task of the translator with it. Literalism in its ideal, utopian form makes the translator disappear so completely behind the words that the reader is given full interpretive freedom, the ability to generate all the meanings, and only those, that were present in the original text and from that array to select those that seem most appropriate ('para que los que leyeren la traducción puedan entender la variedad toda de sentidos á que da ocasión el original si se leyese, y quedan libres para escoger de ellos el que mejor les pareciere'). Whereas the commentator ('el que declara') speaks in his own name and thus puts a textual and interpretive layer over the primary text, obscuring as well as enlightening the reader's view of the source but always interfering in the interpretive process, the word for word translator should ideally be able to present the reader with a painstakingly accurate, unaltered, unadulterated copy of the original, an exact double.

This view neatly circumscribes and delimits the translator's role and responsibilities, in a way that is reminiscent of the statements by Scotus Eriugena's separation of translation and interpretive exposition, and the less sharp distinctions made by Chrysoloras, Madrigal and Erasmus. Between Erasmus and Luis de León there is, moreover, chronologically and geographically speaking, the further figure of Juan Luis Vives. The chapter on translation ('Versiones seu interpretationes') in Vives's *De ratione dicendi* of 1532 is moderate in tone and comes down in favour of 'ad sensum' rather than 'ad verbum' renderings, but it too declares that for certain difficult works like those of Aristotle, and for religious writings and official documents, counting out the words is the best way to proceed because it reduces to a minimum the translator's interpretive intervention and hence his responsibility for the meanings invested in the new text (Coseriu 1971; Vega 1994: 115–18).

To the extent that translation is construed as 'saying the same thing', it appears, literalism constitutes its most secure ideology. It allows the translator to negate his own presence and voice by becoming wholly transparent. This ascetic, sacrificial self-abnegation in turn forms the basis of the reader's trust in the translator as re-enunciator. If interpretive non-intervention is the rule, then any translative mode which detaches itself from the original's words and involves the translator as an interpreting and speaking subject creates room for misinterpretation, distortion, corruption of integrity, betrayal of trust. But the price for purity and rectitude is a text that is hard to read, to the point of unintelligibility, a form of expression that shames the translator, who nonetheless accepts the humiliation in a spirit of self-sacrifice. This is precisely what Jerome's dilemma consisted in: loyalty to the words makes too many and too heavy demands on the reader, but straying from the words is incompatible with the task of the translator, which is an ethical demand to transmit the original whole and unadulterated. In the course of the sixteenth century the dilemma is formulated repeatedly in these terms. As late as 1623 the Dutch writer Constantijn Huygens put it very succinctly: 'If we take liberties in Translating, the truth will suffer; if we keep closely to the words, the spirit of what is said will vanish' ('Neemtmen de ruymte in 't Oversetten, soo kan de waerheid niet vrij van geweld gaen: Staetmen scherp op de woorden, soo verdwijnt de geest vande uytspraeck'; Huygens 1892–1899, I: 284–85).

As far as the literal translators are concerned, 'the truth' takes precedence over 'the spirit of what is said'. That is after all the moral underpinning of their position. It is in the name of truth that they practise their self-denial: transmitting the original intact requires self-restraint and submission. Thus, for instance, the French translator Jacques Gohorry in 1548, in the preface to his version of Livy: he has followed his model as closely as possible, he declares, because his did not want to 'violate or tarnish' its majesty by any 'addition or diminution' coming from his own pen ('. . . suis efforcé de suivre de plus pres qu'il m'a esté possible, estimant telle magesté de dire n'estre a violer ne souiller par addition ou diminution venant du mien'; Norton 1984: 145). Or Denis Sauvage, translating from the Italian in 1551, who ties himself to his original's every word so as not to allow his own spirit to wander in freedom and stray off ('j'ay suyvi ma copie Italienne . . . presque de mot a mot, sans extravaguer, & sans m'égayer en la liberté de mon esprit'; Norton 1984: 146). The Jesuit Andreas Schottus, as we saw, defined the 'faithful translator' in 1610 as one who does not deviate a fingernail's breadth from his author ('Fidus Interpres is demum est, qui ad verbum sic redit, ut ne latum quidem unguem ab auctore . . . discedat') and who does not add, omit or alter anything ('Nonne ad verbum, fide bona, in aliam transfundere linguam, nihil ut de tuo addas, demas nihil, nihil denique immutes'). In England Ben Jonson will support this position: in 1627 Jonson praises a translation 'so wrought / As not the smallest joint or gentlest word / In the great mass or machine there is stirred' (Spingarn 1908, 1: liv).

This again leads into the seventeenth century, when the word for word principle as constituting the law of translation and the duty of the translator is fast losing ground. The pressure has come from different sides, and stems both from vernacular translators increasingly aware of the grammatical and idiomatic differences between languages, and from the Humanist or Humanist-inspired translators with their emphasis on style and rhetorical propriety. The sixteenth-century discourse on translation shows clear traces of this tension. It is evident enough in Joachim du Bellay's dismissal of translation for literary purposes: what he contemptuously called the 'law of translating', a narrowly confined space, was held responsible for texts deemed unpalatable as literature, and writers who wanted to make their mark were advised to turn to imitation rather than translation. Around the same time the translator Jean Lalement, writing in 1549, intends to stay as close as possible to his author Demosthenes, but realizes that such a 'scrupulous' rendering, 'quasi word for word', will not go down well with his readers and land him with the reputation of being 'too religious' a translator, a label he clearly regards as undesirable ('si je l'eusse voulu scrupuleusement translater et quasi de mot à mot, à peine eussé-je esté entendu, et mais reputé trop religieux translateur', Horguelin 1981: 59).

The significance of such a pronouncement lies in the fact that once words like 'scrupulous', 'religious' and other key adjectives in the literalist vocabulary acquire negative connotations, the whole arsenal of terms deployed to justify and sustain the word for word principle comes under threat. This tension can now be recognized as one of the faultlines running through the Renaissance theory of translation. Seen from this perpective it is the presence of a literalist principle which gives the vocabulary of the liberal translators its oppositional, polemical edge, its urgency and relevance. It then becomes clear that with the comments by the rhetorically trained Humanist translators from Gianozzo Manetti and Leonardo Bruni in the fifteenth to Etienne Dolet, Jacques Amyot, Lawrence Humphrey or John Christopherson in the sixteenth century a number of new terms are introduced into the metalanguage of translation which derive their specific thrust and their surplus value from the opposition to the repertoire and the self-justification of the literalists. This is the case with the 'correct way to translate' ('interpretatio recta') of Manetti and Bruni. The emphasis which Bruni's 'De interpretatione recta' of ca. 1425) places on the need for the translator to possess a thorough knowledge and mastery of all the resources of both the original's and the receptor language, on profound familiarity with the original writers and their contexts, on the need for verbal propriety in the translated text and on the preservation of the source text's stylistic power and individuality, all this acquires added force when it is seen against the backdrop of the principle and practice of literalist translation.[8] In the title of Etienne Dolet's 'Manière de bien traduire d'une langue en aultre' of 1540 it is the adverb 'bien' which needs stressing, as its concern with 'translating well' echoes the 'bene dicere', the art of 'well speaking' of the Humanist rhetorical tradition. The 'Manière' does not list a few commonplace rules of thumb, as is sometimes thought, but presents an emphatic image of the ideal rhetorical translator (as indeed Glyn Norton has persuasively argued; see Norton 1974 and 1984). Dolet's explicit rejection of word for word translation in the third of his five points has an obvious focus, but the entire treatise is informed by the polemical opposition to what he sees as the pedestrianism of the literalists. The concern for stylistic quality is evidenced not only in the abundance of terms referring to 'grace', 'majesty', 'dignity', 'richness', 'perfection' 'sweetness', 'harmony of language', 'splendour', 'eloquence' and the 'properties, turns of phrase, expressions, subtleties, and vehemences' of language in what is after all a short text, but also, more than anything else perhaps, in the almost Freudian slip in the final sentence, where, at the end of his fifth and longest point, which deals with rhetorical structures and figures, Dolet seems to have forgotten he is writing about translation and concludes his brief treatise speaking of the 'orator' instead ('Qui sont les poincts d'ung orateur parfaict et vrayment comblé de toute gloire d'éloquence', in Weinberg 1950: 83).

Very much the same stress on the quality of the translating language over and above fidelity to the meaning of the words can be heard in the English Humanist John Christopherson's pronouncements on translation around the mid sixteenth century. When, writing from Louvain in 1553, Christopherson dedicates his Latin translation of four short works by Philo Judaeus to Trinity College, Cambridge, he first defines the task ('munus') of both translator and editor as one of exact rendering of the original's meaning, without addition or deviation: 'in translating as well as in editing ancient writers my principle is, and always has been, not to add anything of my own, not to invent anything, but, when I discharge the duty of a translator, to express truthfully the author's meaning, and when I work as a corrector, to compare carefully the printed copies with the manuscripts' ('Sed mihi certè in veteribus scriptoribus tum convertendis, tum emendandis ea religio & est, &

---

8 For Bruni's treatise, see Baron 1928 (Latin text) and Griffiths et al. 1987 (English translation); short extracts in English also appeared in Lefevere 1992: 82–86. On Manetti, see Norton 1984.

semper fuit, ut nihil de meo addere voluerim, nihil confingere, sed cum munere fungerer interpretis, sententiam authoris verè exprimere, cum autem corrrectoris, exemplaria impressa cum manu descriptis diligenter conferre laborarim'; 1553: b2r°). However, Christopherson goes on, in translating an original that can boast pure diction, stylistic elegance, concise expression and other such qualities, the aim must be to allow the Latin reader to derive as much enjoyment from the Latin rendering as Greek readers do reading the Greek ('tum profectò qui Latina solum fortè lecturi sint, tantum ex illis delectationis caperent, quantum qui Graeca', ibid.: b2v°). This, he adds, he could not quite manage, however hard he tried, nor in his opinion could anyone working only as a translator ('Verum nec poteram, etiam si maximè in illud incubuissem, nec quenquam, qui interpres solum esse voluerit, aliquando efficere posse arbitror'; ibid.: b3r°). For what is required is a text which makes full use of the grammatical and rhetorical resources of the translating language ('Danda tamen est opera ei, qui quempiam scriptorem convertere instituat, ut verbis propriis & aptis ad consuetudinem eius linguae, in quam convertit, utatur'). This means that the translator should avoid two errors above all: first, that of neglecting the original author's sense and meaning in the search for an aesthetically pleasing expression, and secondly, circumlocution, which is the commentator's privilege ('Neque dum sermonis elegantiae student, sensum & sententiam authoris negligat, neque dum partes suscipit interpretis, circuitone, quae es rerum explicatoris propria, utatur: quae duo vitia in vertendo maximè omnium vitanda sunt'; ibid.).

Some fifteen years later, in the 'Translator's Preface' ('Proemium Interpretis') which he attaches to his Latin version of Eusebius' *Historia ecclesiastica* (1569), Christopherson reiterates his exacting vision of a rhetorically adequate translation:

Mihi in convertendis Graecis aciem mentis acrius defigenti quatuor potissimum videntur requiri, vera sensus sententiaeque explicatio, latinitas, numerus, et ea, quam dixi, sermonis perspicuitas. Primum ad fidem, secundum ad delectationem, tertium ad aurium iudicium, quartum ad intelligentiam solet acommodari. [. . .] Quamvis enim in sacris literis interpretandis ordo verborum retinenda est, ut ait D. Hieronymus, quia mysterium est, tamen in aliorum Graecorum interpretatione eodem authore Cicerone et citante et imitante, non verbum e verbo, sed sensus de sensu exprimendus. [. . .] Eloquentia non est illa inanis et prope puerilis verborum volubilitas, quae saepe in populo insolenter se venditat, sed diserte et copiose loquens sapientia, quae in prudentum animos cum suavitate illabitur.

[As I fix the sight of my mind intently on the translation of the Greek, four things in particular seem to be required: a true explanation of sense and meaning, good latinity, harmony, and that perspicuity of speech which I have spoken of. The first is usually held to be relevant for fidelity, the second for delight, the third for the judgment of the ears, the fourth for the understanding [. . .] Although in translating the Scriptures the order of the words should be retained, as St Jerome says, because it is a mystery: yet in the translation of other Greek writings, on the authority of that same Cicero who both cited and imitated them, we should translate not word for word, but meaning for meaning. [. . .] For eloquence is not that empty and almost puerile verbosity which offers itself for sale insolently among the people, but wisdom speaking eloquently and copiously which glides indo the minds of the prudent with sweetness]

(Binns 1978: 135–36)

As around the mid-century such Humanist-inspired, rhetorically adept translators like Amyot, Dolet and Christopherson redefine the field of translation by relocating the boundary markers and repartitioning the allotment, they decisively relegate the word for word principle to the periphery – to the translation of special classes of texts such as the Scriptures or certain pedagogical works. The literal translator's professed love of the naked, unadorned truth comes to be seen as a wrongheaded illusion, which neglects the core essence – force, genius, *esprit*, in short the power of rhetorically effective language – for the mere external husk of the word and its surface meaning. The self-justifying discourse of the literalists is here dismissed from a position of cultural superiority.

The devaluation of the word for word arsenal continues into the seventeenth century. By that time, and beginning with figures like Chapman in England and Malherbe in France, a new, culturally self-conscious generation of vernacular translators has come to the fore. Their repeated rejections of literalism suggest that the idea is still alive, but it has been reduced from a 'religious' faithfulness to a mere 'superstition'. Sir Thomas Elyot declared as early as 1531, with reference to a sermon by Saint Cyprian, that he had 'traunslated this lytell boke: not supersticiousely folowynge the letter . . . but kepynge the sentence and intent of the Authour' (Baumann 1992: 6). In 1616 the academic translator Barten Holyday says he has adopted 'a moderate paraphrase' rather than the 'ferulary superstition to the letter' in rendering the poems of Persius into English (Steiner 1975: 12). In the seventeenth century this is the way the 'libertine' and 'belles infidèles' translators in

England and France routinely use the term. In the preface to his first published translation (1637), Nicolas Perrot d'Ablancourt speaks dismissively of the 'Judaic superstition' of clinging to the words while disregarding the underlying intent and design (Zuber 1972: 111).[9] The positive terms which these translators employ – 'spirit', 'soul', 'life', 'grace', 'elegance', 'eloquence', 'excellencies' etc. (Steiner 1975: 24–25) – are exactly those that were introduced into metatranslational discourse by the Humanists of the fifteenth and sixteenth centuries. They indicate all those qualities which Du Bellay claimed could not possibly be rendered by translators because the 'law of translating' did not allow them the necessary room for manoeuvre.

With the rise of the 'belles infidèles' translators in France and the 'libertine' translators in England, the climate for culturally prestigious translation has shifted decisively away from the literalist principle. When around the mid seventeenth century another generation of French writers and translators begins to speak of the 'rules' of translation (as do, for example, Gaspar Bachet de Méziriac in 1635, Antoine Lemaistre ca. 1650, Gaspard de Tende in 1660; cf. Horguelin 1981: 82, 98, 100), these concepts have not only a different context but also a different basis, being closer to an emerging French Classicist mode of thinking. A different cultural constellation has come into being.

To return to our starting point: if we are to make sense of the different strands of thinking about translation in the sixteenth century, it helps if we can somehow connect them, if we can read and interpret them in relation and in contrast to one another. Clearly, every construction of an overall picture joining together heterogeneous discourses remains just that, a construction. But if we ask ourselves what could be meant,

---

[9] In his edition of d'Ablancourt's prefaces Roger Zuber does not comment on the use of the term 'Judaic'. It seems likely, however, that the explanation for it will be the same as that given by Glyn Norton for the occurrence of a similar reference a century earlier, in a court case of 1534 between the Sorbonne and the *lecteurs royaux* concerning the translation and interpretation of the Bible. There it was alleged that to interpret and translate well one must 'take out the medullary and mystical sense and not adhere to the cortex of words as do the Jews' ('il faut prendre, *sensum medullarem et mysticum, & non reddere verbum verbo, seu adhaerere cortici verborum ut faciunt Iudaei*'). As Norton has shown, the idea that Jewish readings of the Bible followed the letter rather than the (Christian or pre-Christian) spirit is also attested in several fifteenth- and sixteenth-century legal works (Norton 1984: 60–62; 1987: 10). In all probability D'Ablancourt is referring to this traditional perception.

or covered, by terms like 'the law of translation' or the 'office' or 'duty' of the translator, why writers like Dolet or Christopherson appear to state the obvious in urging rhetorically adequate translation, or what it is that the seventeenth-century 'libertine' translators are arguing against, we find ourselves being thrown back time and again on a network of positions, concepts and historical echoes which suggest that writers on translation are aware of other views and approaches, and engage in open or covert debate with one another and with their audiences. In responding to the cultural and socio-political agendas of their respective environments, and in pursuing their own material and symbolic interests, they build alliances and deploy arguments that reverberate across time and space. Much of the debate about the core of the concept of translation, and hence much of the debate about the definition of translation, appears to centre on what constitutes the 'duty' of the translator, ideally and in practice. For an understanding of Renaissance theories of translation as a single if heterogeneous discursive field, then, it will be useful to think of the contributions to that debate as being linked, and to interpret them – to translate, to gloss them – accordingly.

The principle of word for word translation remains associated with both key notions explored here, even though the validity of the literalist idea is never uncontested and becomes increasingly marginal, an ideology in retreat. To the extent that the conflicts between the rhetorical priorities of the Humanist-inspired translators and the literalist concerns of the more traditional translators are focused on exactly what constitutes the translator's duty, however, the exploration of this cluster of key terms together with their reverberations back and forth in time seems likely to take us to the heart of those debates. Insofar as literalism is associated with the 'law' of translation and the 'duty' of the translator, it provides a privileged way into these discussions. That is what this essay set out to show.

Works Cited

Allan, P.S. 1906. (Ed.) *Opus epistolarum Des. Erasmi*. Vol. 1. Oxford: Clarendon.

Baron, Hans. 1928. *Leonardi Bruni Aretino. Humanistisch-philosophische Schriften mit einer Chronologie seiner Werke und Briefe*. Leipzig/Berlin: B.G. Teubner.

Baumann, Uwe. 1992. 'Sir Thomas Elyot als Übersetzer: Übersetzungtheorie und Übersetzungspraxis im englischen Frühumanismus'. Herwig Friedl, et al. (ed.), *Literaturübersetzen: Englisch*. Tübingen: Gunter Narr. 3–26.

Bellay, Joachim du. 1931. *Œuvres poétiques*. Ed. Henri Chamard. Paris: Droz.

Bellay, Joachim du. 1948. *La Deffence et illustration de la langue francoyse* [1549]. Ed. Henri Chamard. Paris: Didier.

Binns, J.W. 1978. 'Latin Translations from Greek in the English Renaissance', *Humanistica Lovaniensia*, 27, 128–59.

Christopherson, John [transl.]. 1553. *Philonis Iudaei . . . libri quatuor . . . iam primum de Graeco in Latinum conversi: Ioanne Christophorsono Anglo, interprete*. Antwerp: Johannes Verwithagen.

Copeland, Rita. 1991. *Rhetoric, Hermeneutics, and Translation in the Middle Ages*. Cambridge: Cambridge University Press.

Coseriu, Eugenio. 1971. 'Das Problem des Übersetzens bei Juan Luis Vives'. K. Bausch and H. Gauger (eds), *Interlinguistica*. Tübingen: Niemeyer. 571–82.

Griffiths, Gordon, et al. 1987. (Eds) *The Humanism of Leonardo Bruni. Selected Texts*. Binghamton: Medieval & Renaissance Texts & Studies.

Hermans, Theo. 1992. 'Renaissance Translation between Literalism and Imitation'. Harald Kittel (ed.), *Geschichte, System, literarische Übersetzung / Histories, Systems, Literary Translations*. Berlin: Erich Schmidt. 95–116.

Hermans, Theo. 1996. (Ed.) *Door eenen engen hals. Nederlandse beschouwingen over vertalen 1550–1670*. The Hague: Stichting Bibliographia Neerlandica.

Horatius, Quintus Flaccus. 1594. *Quincti Horatii Flacci . . . Poemata omnia*. Leyden: Franciscus Raphelengius.

Horguelin, Paul. 1981. (Ed.) *Anthologie de la manière de traduire*. Montréal: Linguatech.

Hoskin, Keith. 1985. '*Verbum de verbo*: The Perennial Changing Paradox of Translation'. Theo Hermans (ed.), *Second Hand*. Antwerp: ALW. 10–45.

Huygens, Constantijn. 1892–99. *De gedichten van Constantijn Huygens*. Ed. J.A. Worp. 9 vols. Groningen: Wolters.

Jerome, Saint. 1953. *Lettres*, vol. III. Ed. J. Labourt. Paris: Les belles lettres.

Keightley, R.G. 1977. 'Alfonso de Madrigal and the *Chronici Canones* of Eusebius', *The Journal of Medieval and Renaissance Studies* 7, 2, 225–48.

Lefevere, André. 1992. (Ed.) *Translation/History/Culture, A Sourcebook*. London/New York: Routledge.

López García, Dámaso. 1996. (Ed.) *Teorías de la Traducción. Antología de textos*. Cuenca: Eds. de la Universidad de Castilla-La Mancha.

Norton, Glyn. 1974. 'Translation Theory in Renaissance France: Etienne Dolet and the Rhetorical Tradition', *Renaissance and Reformation* 10, 1–13.

Norton, Glyn. 1984. *The Ideology and Language of Translation in Renaissance France and their Humanist Antecedents*. Genève: Droz.

Norton, Glyn. 1987. 'The Politics of Translation in early Renaissance France: Confrontations of Policy and Theory during the Reign of Francis I'. Brigitte Schultze (ed.), *Die literarische Übersetzung. Fallstudien zu ihrer Kulturgeschichte*. Berlin: Erich Schmidt. 1–13.

Peletier du Mans, Jacques. 1990. *Art poétique* [1555]. F. Goyet (red.), *Traités de poétique et de rhétorique de la Renaissance*. Paris: Librairie Générale Française. 235–324.

Rener, Frederick. 1989. *Interpretatio. Language and Translation from Cicero to Tytler*. Amsterdam: Rodopi.

Santoyo, Julio-César. 1987. (Ed.) *Teoría y crítica de la traducción. Antología*. Bellaterra: Universitat Autónoma de Barcelona.

Schottus, Andreas. 1610. *Tullianarum Quaestionum De instaurando Ciceronis Imitatione Libri IIII*. Antwerp: Jan Moretus.

Schwarz, Werner. 1985. *Schriften zur Bibelübersetzung und zur mittelalterlichen Übersetzungstheorie*. London: Institute of Germanic Studies.

Spingarn, J.E. 1908. (Ed.) *Critical Essays of the Seventeenth Century*. 3 vols. Oxford: Clarendon.

Steiner, T.R. 1975. (Ed.) *English Translation Theory 1650–1800*. Assen/Amsterdam: Van Gorcum.

Sturrock, John. 1990. 'Writing Between the Lines: The Language of Translation'. *New Literary History* 21, 4, 993–1013.

Vega, Miguel Ángel. 1994. (Ed.) *Textos clásicos de teoría de la traducción*. Madrid: Cátedra.

Weinberg, Bernard. 1950. *Critical Prefaces of the French Renaissance*. Evanston, Ill.: Northwestern University Press.

Zuber, Roger. 1972. (Ed.) *Nicolas Perrot D'Ablancourt. Lettres et préfaces critiques*. Paris: Marcel Didier.

Heroic Couplet Translation –
a Unique Solution?

FELICITY ROSSLYN

WHAT DOES THE MODERN READER expect of a translation? Chiefly, that it should read easily, and be accurate, expressing only what the author intended. We cheerfully buy our paperback Homer, Virgil or Bible on the assumption that these are the real thing, or very nearly so; and we leave older translations, in less accessible idioms, on the library shelf.

The preference for 'natural' sounding translation, and the presumption that 'accuracy' is the essence of the translator's task, are so universal now that it comes as a surprise to discover that these attitudes have a precise historical date to them – and before that time, virtually the opposite understanding prevailed. In the lifetime of Dryden and Pope (the hundred years from 1640–1740, say) translation was something that possessed an idiom of its own, and accuracy was the least of the translator's obligations: he was required to reproduce the greatness of his original, by whatever means he could. But by the 1760s dissenting voices were heard, and by the time of Cowper's *Iliad* in 1791, literal accuracy had become the aim.[1] Cowper rejected the heroic couplet idiom of his predecessors precisely because it could not be accurate: the obligation to rhyme and employ heroic vocabulary were now insuperable barriers. His own translation was in blank verse; and it set the stage for Coleridge's denunciation of Pope's Homer in *Biographia Literaria* as 'the main source of our pseudo-poetic diction'[2] – a position that hardened into Romantic orthodoxy and has not really been displaced in our time.

The aim of this essay is to get behind the barrier that stands between us and heroic couplet translations. Taking Pope's *Iliad* (1715–20) as a key example, it tries to uncover Pope's way of working and suggest how his translation would have sounded to its Augustan audience – among them Doctor Johnson, who famously thought it 'a performance which

---

[1] The classic analysis of this shift and its implications is by H.A. Mason, *To Homer Through Pope* (London: Chatto and Windus, 1972), pp. 61–85.
[2] *Biographia Literaria* (London: 1817), I, p. 39.

no age or nation can pretend to equal'.[3] The main point it attempts to make is that the Romantic orthodoxy about translation that starts with Cowper is actually much less sophisticated than the view it displaced – and that it was precisely its attractive appeal to 'naturalness' that was its undoing. But there are two other ideas related to this which it may be useful to sketch at the beginning (they are of their nature unprovable, but they are worth entertaining). One is that it is not absurd to say that the heroic couplet is as close as English ever came to the Homeric hexameter: in terms of formulaic structure and the generations of bards or poets who formed them, they are surprisingly comparable. The other is that once the couplet was rejected by translators, the baby turned out to have gone with the bathwater; and the nineteenth century is not an age of great translations, not only because it no longer seemed 'creative' enough to rework the past, but because no-one could do it convincingly.[4]

If we are to get round the barrier between us and the heroic couplet, we need to begin by acknowledging the size of it. A large element is the artificiality of the language and structures: clearly, this is not poetry in the sense of 'spontaneous overflow', but poetry in the original Greek sense of *poesis*, 'something made'. It reveals the literariness of literature at every turn, and without any apparent embarrassment: Johnson comments, for instance, that Pope's 'chief help' in his *Iliad* was Dryden's *Aeneid*, and that Pope 'searched the pages of Dryden for happy combinations of heroic diction', as if this method of proceeding did him nothing but credit.[5] To get back to Johnson's way of reading, we clearly have to suspend for a while any Keatsian revulsion we might feel at the construction of verse from formulae and rhymes. For Keats, this debased poetry to mere carpentry; any 'dolt' of Pope's generation (he says scornfully) could be taught

> to smooth, inlay, and clip, and fit,
> Till, like the certain wands of Jacob's wit,
> Their verses tallied. Easy was the task:

3 *Lives of the Poets* (London: Crocker, 1868), p. 426.
4 Arnold must have been the most promising translator among Victorian classicists, but the sophistication of his theoretical views is in painful contrast to his practice, where he persists in trying to create an English hexameter: see his examples in the Oxford lectures *On Translating Homer* (1861).
5 *Lives of the Poets*, p. 427.

A thousand handicraftsmen wore the mask
Of Poesy.[6]

But while no-one would demur that smoothing, clipping and fitting are
necessary skills, it does not follow that 'easy was the task'. While
practice might make for facility, it was never easy to write couplets that
actually meant what the author intended; and the first benefit of
reading widely in the period is distinguishing between authors who say
what they mean, and those who say what they must.

We might measure the difference between 'handicraft' and art by a
glance at Boswell's journal for 1763. As a young man, he set himself
various tasks of self-improvement, and for a short while he practised
two skills every day: writing a short essay in French, and writing ten
lines of verse. His first effort displays both the theory (anyone can write
couplets) and the drawbacks (good couplets require work) with disarm-
ing clarity:

> Ten lines a day I task myself to write,
> Be fancy clouded or be fancy bright,
> Sure, no Egyptian task; for unconfin'd
> Let Genius range the forest of the mind,
> And, as Apollo grants him vigour, grub
> The tow'ring cedar or the lowly shrub.
> I seek not sallies elegant and terse,
> But to acquire the power of making verse;
> And sure by practice I may freely hope
> To turn a line like Dryden or like Pope.[7]

Certainly he may 'freely hope' that practice will eventually allow him
to 'turn a line like Dryden or like Pope'; but until he stops padding his
verse with superfluities like 'freely' and mixing linguistic registers (so
that 'Genius' must 'grub'), he will remain an amateur among profes-
sionals: the poet needs self-criticism just as much as facility.

The intense 'literariness' of the heroic couplet is perhaps easier to
understand if we remember how these poets were taught, by methods
that had barely changed since the Renaissance. An education that
took place in two dead languages had obvious drawbacks, but two

---

6 *Sleep and Poetry*, lines 197–201.
7 *Boswell in Holland 1763–1764*, ed. Frederick Pottle (London: Heinemann,
1952), p. 36.

paradoxical advantages. One was that it involved translation at every turn; and the other was that it widened the issue of translation beyond language, to culture itself. No-one studying Latin as well as Greek could fail to notice how deliberately Roman cultural life was based on Greek (or indeed, how public school culture was based on both). And the school curriculum enforced this discovery in detail. A boy at Westminster School in the seventeenth century, as Dryden was, had to make up Greek and Latin hexameters extempore, on any given theme. This was only possible, not by inventing new verses, but by cobbling together bits of familiar ones; and however dire the results, the boys found themselves practising precisely the method of 'clipping and fitting' that had enabled Virgil or Apollonius to build so much out of Homer. At another time of the day, the challenge would be to turn Greek or Latin poetry into English verse; and the boys reached for their 'cribs' in much the same spirit as the professional translators of the age, not so much to find out what the lines meant, as how to express them in English. When they knew how the lines had been translated last, they constructed a version for themselves; translation in such a context was self-evidently a serial effort, in which expression counted for as much as accuracy.[8]

From a Keatsian perspective this education is distressingly formalist and inauthentic, and it is easy to concede that most boys will have passed through it more whipped than enlightened. But it is hard to imagine a better education for a poet. For whatever the method lacks in flexibility it makes up in sophistication: it is squarely based on the assumption that literature is born of other literature, and that all words have known origins. The method is also sophisticated about the relations between translation and culture: for it exposes the truth that all cultures are continually in a state of translating ('bringing across') what they need from other cultures, and what happened in the (classic) past is still happening in the (English) present. Above all, and perhaps most unpleasantly to Romantic feelings, it accepts that the most successful translation will be the result of a serial effort. Each translator has the work of all his predecessors in his mind's eye, and this is not a condemnation of his powers but the precondition of his success. He works inside

---

8 *Memoir of Richard Busby D.D. (1606–95) with Some Account of Westminster School in the Seventeenth Century* (London: Lawrence and Bullen, 1895), pp. 78–80.

the translating idiom he has inherited and makes it mean all that it can; he finishes what others made possible.[9]

With these thoughts in mind, we can turn to Pope's method of working in his *Iliad* translation Book I (1715) and note with less surprise that his editors have found traces of his reading of the same book in Chapman (1611), Ogilby (1660), Hobbes (1676), Dryden (1700), Maynwaring (1704) and an English translation from the French (1712) – aside from all the learned authorities and annotators he consulted on matters of detail.[10] These six versions range from the admirable (Dryden at his most mature) to the comically inept (the philosopher Hobbes is no poet) with much banality in between; but the overall value of the versions is not relevant to Pope. He looks at them for turns of phrase, rhymes, epithets and promptings of every kind, which Hobbes can supply as well as the best; for what Pope brings to the process (and what Keats feared was missing) is poetic judgment. He decides what to put in and what to take out: in the effort to make the idiom mean all that it can, blunders can be as helpful as glowing examples. If we take a close look at the opening of Book I we can watch this serial effort in slow motion. Let us take Dryden's version first, and comparing it with Pope's, try to look at it through his eyes:

> The wrath of *Peleus'* son, O Muse, resound;
> whose dire effects the *Grecian* army found,
> And many a Heroe, King, and hardy Knight,
> Were sent, in early Youth, to Shades of night:
> Their Limbs a Prey to Dogs and Vulturs made;
> So was the Sov'reign Will of *Jove* obey'd:
> From that ill-omen'd Hour when Strife begun,
> Betwixt *Atrides* Great, and *Thetis'* god-like Son. (1–8)

Dryden's majestic competence is so evident that it is hard to see how this might be improved on until we compare it with Pope's. But the younger poet's admiration for his mentor clearly did not prevent him from aiming for something better. Strictly speaking, 'resound/found' is somewhat forced, and 'begun/Son' is pedestrian; the important verbs

---

[9] The process is perhaps less unfamiliar than it seems: we take it for granted that the Authorised Version of the Bible is largely based on Tyndale and Coverdale, and it is known that Tyndale read closely in Luther and Erasmus.
[10] *Twickenham Edition of the Works of Alexander Pope* (London and New Haven: Methuen, 1967), VII–VIII, Introduction, pp. lxxi–clxiii, and appendix F (vol. X). Hereafter *TE*.

are all passive ('were sent', 'were made', 'was obey'd') and the 'hardy Knights' are distractingly chivalric for the context. Pope's 1715 version tries for something more energetic, and stylistically more of a piece:

> The Wrath of *Peleus*' Son, the direful Spring
> Of all the *Grecian* Woes, O Goddess, sing!
> That Wrath which hurl'd to *Pluto*'s gloomy Reign
> The Souls of mighty Chiefs untimely slain;
> Whose Limbs unbury'd on the naked Shore
> Devouring Dogs and hungry Vultures tore.
> Since Great *Achilles* and *Atrides* strove,
> Such was the Sov'reign Doom, and such the Will of *Jove*.
>
> (1–8)

Now the verbs are dramatically active ('hurl'd') and pushed to the end of the line to energise the couplets ('tore', 'strove'); the epic atmosphere is unmistakable ('direful Spring', 'untimely slain') and the shade of Milton is lightly evoked by delaying the first verb 'sing' to the second line – a reminder of the six lines we are kept waiting by *Paradise Lost*. (The translation is full of such evocations, not only of Milton, but Ovid, Virgil and the Bible.)

Only two days after Pope published this, another *Iliad* Book I appeared as a deliberate challenge: this was by Thomas Tickell, hoping to undermine Pope's subscription. Tickell's version was politically rather than poetically motivated, and it sank without trace, but it gives us a useful opportunity to compare this translating idiom in the hands of someone merely competent, as opposed to a real poet. It also reveals Pope's sense of his own standards: his personal copy is covered in furious annotations. In Tickell's version, written without sight of Pope's but clearly with Dryden in view, we can see how high is the general level of facility in turning couplets among the classically educated. At the same time, there is no mistaking a lower poetic temperature; one would not wish to read a great deal of such verse:

> *Achilles*' fatal Wrath, whence Discord rose,
> That brought the Sons of *Greece* unnumber'd Woes,
> O Goddess sing. Full many a Hero's Ghost
> Was driv'n untimely to th'Infernal Coast,
> While in promiscuous Heaps their Bodies lay,
> A Feast for Dogs, and ev'ry Bird of Prey.
> So did the Sire of Gods and Men fulfill
> His steadfast Purpose, and Almighty Will;

What time the haughty Chiefs their Jars begun,
Atrides King of Men, and *Peleus'* godlike Son.   (1–10)

Tickell is aiming to sound poetic, but creating technical problems for himself. Like Pope, he feels invocations after *Paradise Lost* should be Miltonic, but in postponing 'O Goddess sing' until line three, he writes a Miltonic half-line and creates a caesura that arrests the flow. He is trying to write blank verse inside a couplet: 'O Goddess sing. Full many a Hero's Ghost . . .' The passive cast of the verbs in Dryden's version leads him into similarly weak constructions ('was driv'n', 'in Heaps . . . lay') and Dryden also tempts him into a mixture of epic diction and colloquialism that in Tickell sounds merely odd ('what time the haughty Chiefs their Jars began' – Dryden uses 'jar', and squabble, later on in the book for comic effect, but 'what time' is a conspicuous Miltonism).

This much we may see for ourselves, but if we look at the annotations to Pope's own copy, we can also see what struck his arch-critical eye.[11] He marks this couplet for bad grammar, for instance:

So did the Sire of Gods and Men fulfill
His steadfast Purpose, and Almighty Will.   (7–8)

In Pope's book one may 'fulfill' a 'Purpose' but not a 'Will'; the right way to phrase this would be as he does some years later, in his *Odyssey* XI:

Won by prophetic knowledge, to fulfill
The stedfast Purpose of th'Almighty will.   (363–4)

Pope also marks the rhyme 'begun/Son' with 'Chapman': this dull rhyme owes its existence in both Tickell and Dryden to Chapman's version of 1611. He underlines 'did' in 'So did the Sire of Gods' as the kind of prosaic padding all couplet writers should resist, and gives 'A Feast for Dogs' and 'Jars' his mark for incongruous vocabulary that spoils the epic atmosphere. To Pope's eye, Tickell's verse, competent as it is, is not built to endure wind and weather; it is miscellaneous and uncontrolled, pointing in different directions at the same time.

The level of interrelation and mutual scrutiny between these three

---

[11] A full account is given in the author's 'Pope's Annotations to Tickell's *Iliad* Book One', *Review of English Studies* XXX no. 117, pp. 4–59.

versions is perhaps already surprising enough, but a still more suggestive consequence followed from Pope's work on Tickell's *Iliad* – which is that he later modified his own in the light of it. The man who wrote in the *Essay on Criticism*,

> Trust not your self; but your Defects to know,
> Make use of ev'ry *Friend* – and ev'ry *Foe*,   (213–14)

was willing to learn even from a rival, and the serial effort did not come to an end with the first edition. Pope came to think that the clarity of Tickell's opening emphasis on Achilles' name was preferable to his own '*Peleus*' Son', and that Tickell's 'unnumber'd Woes' was finer than 'all the *Grecian* Woes', so in 1736 he rewrote his opening:

> Achilles' Wrath, to Greece the direful spring
> Of Woes unnumber'd, heav'nly Goddess, sing!   (1–2)

Now that we are perhaps close enough to the heroic couplet to see over the barrier – farther, at least, than Keats – the thing that strikes us most is the density of the translating idiom. It is made up of diction generated by hacks and dunces as well as poets; it is a vast repertoire of possibilities available to anyone who reads, and what distinguishes the professional from the amateur is not the kind of verse he writes, but its accuracy. The key signs are unforced rhymes, in which the poet says what he wants to say, not what he is constrained to do; coherent tone; and energy, whereby the poet shows that obeying the rules has not dampened his powers – in accordance with Pope's own maxim in the *Essay on Criticism*,

> True Ease in Writing comes by Art, not Chance,
> As those move easiest who have learn'd to dance.   (362–3)

The whole phenomenon of the serial effort at translating Homer in the early 1700s raises the suggestive possibility that great translations, particularly great translations in poetry, do not come out of nowhere, but need to be supported by a lot of other contemporary attempts. An isolated achievement like Chapman's Homer (1611–15) may seem to contradict this: but the idiosyncrasies of that version, which is stubbornly wrong as often as it is heroically right, are perhaps the price Chapman paid for his solitary eminence. Certainly their knowledgeable audience seems to have been what imparted to Dryden and Pope their discipline and sense of standards. The translator in their day was not an expert delivering his interpretation *de haut en bas*, knowing that no-one could contradict him, but a worker among fellow-workers who could estimate what he did well enough, even if they could not do it themselves. Dryden's and Pope's translations were the perfection of something being practised just as optimistically by a Tickell.

If we note this community of effort as one unique aspect of the period's translations, another may be the sophisticated reading habits produced by a classical education. As we have already seen, schoolboys who built so naturally on the work of others were bound to observe the same process going on in the literature of the past. Their training made them hypersensitive to the construction and content of the literary genres: in the case of the epic, to the way Virgil had built the *Aeneid* out of carefully selected parts of the *Iliad* and *Odyssey*, and Milton had made *Paradise Lost* by inserting all three into the framework of Genesis. They heard a perpetual conversation going on between the present and the past, and read their classics in the light of the literature the classics themselves had given rise to. A small example of the readiness to assume a mutuality between the literature of the past and the present has already been given, in the way neither Pope nor Tickell could imagine writing a non-Miltonic invocation after *Paradise Lost*. To the modern objection that this was not Homeric, and the role of the translator was to be faithful to his author, they would probably have answered that the translator's prime obligation was to write English – an English that conveyed the epic quality of the original as credibly as possible. Since Milton was the ultimate source of that credibility in the early 1700s, to be Miltonic *was* to be Homeric.

A striking example of this theory can be found in Book XXI of Pope's *Iliad*, and it may be worth examining in detail, since it shows what the dense fabric of this translating idiom could be made to do, in the hands of a master. It comes from the climax of a speech made by Achilles to a captive Trojan prince, whom he is on the point of slaughtering in defiance of the Homeric code. Achilles, maddened by the death of Patroclus, tells him sardonically to prepare to die; supplication will do him no good whatever:

> Now it is your turn to die. Why complain, my friend? Patroclus has died, who was a much better man than you; and tall and strong as I am, son of a mortal and a goddess, I too am under sentence of death.
> (*Iliad*, XXI 106–10)

In Pope's version, this speech reaches the reader via Ennius, Lucretius and Dryden – not randomly, but deliberately, since Lucretius evoked these words of Achilles in *De Rerum Natura*, and Dryden is the author who has most recently turned Lucretius into English. Pope is therefore paying Homer back in his own coin in this version, returning to the epic the resonance it has itself generated:

> Talk not of Life, or Ransom, (he replies)
> *Patroclus* dead, whoever meets me, dies:
> In vain a single *Trojan* sues for Grace;
> But least, the Sons of *Priam*'s hateful Race.
> Die then, my Friend! what boots it to deplore?
> The great, the good *Patroclus* is no more!
> He, far thy Better, was fore-doom'd to die,
> 'And thou, dost thou, bewail Mortality.'   (XXI 111–18)

This last line is actually a direct quotation from Dryden's Lucretius, as the quotation marks acknowledge; but the whole passage is suffused with the philosophical spirit of *De Rerum Natura*, where Lucretius boldly satirises the individual's shivering apprehension of his own mortality. 'Consider', says Lucretius, 'why *you* should be exempt. Great kings, heroic warriors, famous philosophers and artists have died, and Homer himself.' Invoking a line of the same kind from Ennius' *Annales* ('postquam lumina sis oculis bonus Ancu' reliquit', 154), Lucretius rewrites Achilles' phrasing about Patroclus:

> Hoc etiam tibi tute interdum dicere possis:
> 'lumina sis oculis etiam bonus Ancu' reliquit,
> qui melior multis quam tu fuit, improbe, rebus.'
>
> (III 1024–6)

Dryden translated this section of the poem as one of the most famous of all atheist statements, under the title 'Against the Fear of Death' (1685); and here the key lines appear as,

> Meantime, when thoughts of death disturb thy head;
> Consider, *Ancus*, great and good, is dead;
> *Ancus*, thy better far, was born to die;
> And thou, dost thou bewail mortality?   (236–9)

Pope's manuscript shows that he originally translated this passage with the quotation in a submerged state, perhaps not aware of the source of the phrases his memory had supplied him with:

The great, ye good Patroclus dyd before
Patroclus, much thy Better, sunk by fate
& thou, does thou, lament thy mortal State?

(BL Add. MS 4808)

When he realised that 'the great, ye good' and 'thou, does thou' were echoes of Dryden, Pope seems to have revised his phrasing and made the debt visible with quotation marks. 'You know this speech', he implicitly tells the reader; 'you have caught it reverberating down two millennia':

The great, the good *Patroclus* is no more!
He, far thy Better, was fore-doom'd to die,
'And thou, dost thou, bewail Mortality?'

The reader is invited to read Homer in the light of the literature he has given rise to; the classic is not the unreachable 'other' but the Father of (western) Poetry, the most familiar presence of all.

This is one small example of a widespread phenomenon. When Pope reaches a simile used by Virgil in the *Georgics*, he reinvokes it, often with reference to Dryden's translation; when he comes to a passage reworked in *Paradise Lost*, he gives his translation a Miltonic colouring; Lucretius, Ovid, and even Pope's original poetry are similarly invoked. There seem to be two motives at work: one is that Pope himself cannot read Homer without being reminded of all the later literature he has generated, so that the act of translation is also an act of commentary – 'reception theory' before its time. The other is a spirit of practical economy: Homer, like any author, loses so much in translation that he must be repaid by any means available. If Virgil, Milton or Dryden can show Pope how to make his original 'shine' in English, their help is to be gladly used; it is a variant of the same practicality that borrows English diction from Tickell.

One problem for the modern reader is the difficulty of responding to such a high level of allusiveness. Are we to read all the literature the *Iliad* has generated before we are qualified to read this translation? How are we to feel when Pope persistently reminds us of literary experiences that, thanks to a modern education, we have not had? It must be acknowledged that we are not in a position to catch his direct allusions: these must now reach us via footnotes, if at all. But the situation is not desperate; for Pope's technique is much more often one of generalised allusiveness, where a sensitive reader is required to respond to the spirit and tone of the poetry, without being precisely aware of its elements or origin. Just as no-one but Pope and Tickell would have been aware of how much Dryden and Milton went into their Book I invocations, so no-one but Pope (and later on, his editors) could identify precisely which elements were animating particular passages. The Augustan reader would respond to the effect in the poetry, and the modern reader is not debarred from doing the same.

An interesting example of this submerged allusiveness follows the speech of Achilles in Book XXI we have been looking at. The key event in this book is the struggle between the River Xanthus and Achilles. It is one of Homer's most dramatic fictions: Achilles is throwing the bodies of slaughtered Trojans into the river, and as the carcases begin to choke its flow the river rises up to avenge itself. It comes so close to overwhelming and drowning the hero that Hera intervenes and begs the god of fire, Hephaistos, to fight the river off. He sets fire to the plain and brings the river to the boil; at which point it begs for mercy, capitulates, and flows quietly again in its bed.

This episode exemplifies two things about Homer that were close to Pope's heart. One is that 'he had the greatest Invention of any Writer whatever':

> It is to the Strength of this amazing Invention we are to attribute that unequal'd Fire and Rapture, which is so forcible in *Homer*, that no Man of a true Poetical Spirit is Master of himself while he reads him. What he writes is of the most animated Nature imaginable; every thing moves, every thing lives, and is put in Action. (Preface)[12]

The obligation of the translator is 'above all things to keep alive that Spirit and Fire' (VII, 22). The second conviction is that Homer already has implicit in him the later literary genres (the pastoral in the pastoral similes, satire in the speech of Thersites):

> 'Tis like a copious Nursery which contains the Seeds and first Productions of every kind, out of which those who follow'd him have but selected some particular Plants, each according to his Fancy, to cultivate and beautify. (VII, 3)

What this river-fight represents is the 'seed' of Ovid's *Metamorphoses* — where indeed it partially reappears as the same river being scorched by Phaeton's chariot in Book II.

---

[12] *TE*, VII, 4.

With these thoughts in mind, that the vitality of this episode is essential, and that the Ovidian pleasure in witnessing a metamorphosis – the discovery of a god in a river which subsides back again into inanimate water – is to be had here too, Pope can overcome the resistance he feels, and expects the rational reader to feel, to what is excessively 'marvellous' in this passage. He translates it with a confident verve in which he reaches out, as usual, to Milton, Dryden and Virgil, wherever these are appropriate, but most comprehensively to Ovid. The result is not an 'allusion' to the *Metamorphoses*, but a re-creation, through what Ovid has helped Pope to understand.

Pope's first concern is to convey Achilles' desperate struggle with the water, in language that does justice to the versification of the Greek. It is a challenge to make the sound of his verse an 'echo' to the sense:

> Then rising in his Rage above the Shores,
> From all his Deeps the bellowing River roars,
> Huge Heaps of Slain disgorges on the Coast,
> And round the Banks the ghastly Dead are tost.
> While all before, the Billows rang'd on high
> (A wat'ry Bulwark) screen the Bands who fly.
> Now bursting on his Head with thund'ring Sound,
> The falling Deluge whelms the Hero round:
> His loaded Shield bends to the rushing Tide;
> His Feet, upborn, scarce the strong Flood divide,
> Slidd'ring, and stagg'ring. On the Border stood
> A spreading Elm, that overhung the Flood;
> He seiz'd a bending Bough, his Steps to stay;
> The Plant uprooted to his Weight gave way,
> Heaving the Bank, and undermining all;
> Loud flash the Waters to the rushing Fall
> Of the thick Foliage. The large Trunk display'd
> Bridg'd the rough Flood across: The Hero stay'd
> On this his Weight, and rais'd upon his Hand,
> Leap'd from the Chanel, and regain'd the Land.
> (XXI 257–76)

Pope imitates Achilles' desperate stumbling with enjambment and a clumsy hiatus, and the falling elm crashes down audibly to a firm caesura, as he strives to do justice to his admired original:

> His feet, upborn, scarce the strong Flood divide,
> Slidd'ring, and stagg'ring . . .
> The Plant uprooted to his Weight gave way,

> Heaving the Bank, and undermining all;
> Loud flash the Waters to the rushing Fall
> Of the thick Foliage.   (266–7, 270–3)

He adds a note:

> There is a great Beauty in the Versification of this whole Passage in *Homer*: Some of the Verses run hoarse, full, and sonorous, like the Torrent they describe; others by their broken Cadences, and sudden Stops, image the Difficulty, Labour, and Interruption of the Hero's March against it. The fall of the Elm, the tearing up of the Bank, the rushing of the Branches in the Water, are all put into such Words, that almost every Letter corresponds in its Sound, and echoes to the Sense of each particular. (XXI 262n.)

For the vocabulary, as opposed to the versification, Pope's mind has gone back to another picture of heroic helplessness. The suggestive 'slidd'ring and stagg'ring' recall the unforgettable description of Priam being hauled by Pyrrhus to his own altar for slaughter in Dryden's *Aeneid*, the sole use of the word in the entire poem:

> Now dye: With that he dragg'd the trembling Sire,
> Slidd'ring through clotter'd Blood, and holy Mire.
>   (II 748–9)

And Dryden's evocation of drunkenness in the *Georgics* also showed Pope how to convey staggers through alliteration and strongly accented present participles:

> . . . *Lagaean* Juice,
> Will stamm'ring Tongues, and stagg'ring Feet produce.
>   (II 132–3)

As Achilles escapes it is Milton that comes to Pope's mind:

> Far as a Spear can fly, *Achilles* springs
> At every Bound; His clanging Armour rings:
> Now here, now there, he turns on ev'ry side,
> And winds his Course before the following Tide;
> The Waves flow after, wheresoe'er he wheels,
> And gather fast, and murmur at his Heels.   (283–8)

In Homer the river 'flowed noisily behind', but Pope conveys its swift menace through the motion of Milton's Cherubim, expelling Adam and Eve from Eden. They press behind the culprits as 'fast' as a mist 'gathers' at 'the Labourers heel':

> Gliding meteorous, as Ev'ning Mist
> Ris'n from a River o're the marish glides,
> And gathers ground fast at the Labourers heel
> Homeward returning.   (*Paradise Lost*, XII 629–32)

And Homer's own comparison of Xanthus to a stream of water in an irrigation channel, which goes so fast it even outstrips the farmer controlling it, becomes in Pope's version a miniature pastoral: as he enthusiastically notes,

> This changing of the Character is very beautiful: No Poet ever knew, like *Homer*, to pass from the vehement and the nervous, to the gentle and the agreeable; such Transitions, when properly made, give a singular Pleasure, as when in Musick a Master passes from the rough to the tender. (XXI 289n.)

> > So when a Peasant to his Garden brings
> > Soft Rills of Water from the bubbling Springs,
> > And calls the Floods from high, to bless his Bow'rs
> > And feed with pregnant Streams the Plants and Flow'rs;
> > Soon as he clears whate'er their passage staid,
> > And marks the future Current with his Spade,
> > Swift o'er the rolling Pebbles, down the Hills
> > Louder and louder purl the falling Rills,
> > Before him scatt'ring, they prevent his pains,
> > And shine in mazy Wand'rings o'er the Plains.   (289–98)

Because he understands the function of this simile to be a glimpse of beauty in the midst of horror, Pope suppresses the farmer's surprise at the stream's rapidity in favour of the water's alacrity to co-operate: the 'falling Rills . . . prevent his pains/ And shine in mazy Wand'rings o'er the Plains.' But the conversion of this simile into pastoral is not Pope's invention: Virgil did it before him by inserting the passage into the *Georgics*, as Pope reminds the reader by quoting it in at the end of the footnote above (XXI 289n.). In the *Georgics* it is Virgil's poetical guide to irrigation:

> deinde satis fluvium inducit rivosque sequentis
> et, cum exustus ager morientibus aestuat herbis,

ecce supercilio clivosi tramitis undam
elicit? illa cadens raucum per levia murmur
saxa ciet scatebrisque arentia temperat arva.   (106–10)

It is Dryden's translation of this advice that gives Pope his 'calls the
Floods from high' and 'pregnant Streams':

And call the floods from high, to rush amain
With pregnant Streams, to swell the teeming Grain.
                                                        (I 155–6)

The hero calls aloud to the gods to save him from the ignominy of
drowning, and receives their welcome assurance that this is not to be
his fate. He heaves himself out of the river to return to the massacre –
at which point the river becomes incensed beyond bearing, and the
poetry takes on an Ovidian vitality. Xanthus is speaking:

No Hand his Bones shall gather, or inhume;
These his cold Rites, and this his wat'ry Tomb.
    He said; and on the Chief descends amain,
Increas'd with Gore, and swelling with the Slain.
Then murm'ring from his Beds, he boils, he raves,
And a Foam whitens on the purple Waves.
At ev'ry Step, before Achilles stood
The crimson Surge, and delug'd him with Blood.   (376–83)

Pope is striving to do justice to Homer's 'Living Words' (VII 10) by
writing with as much metaphorical energy as possible. The anthropomorphic cast of his verbs ('swelling . . . he raves') makes the 'Foam'
seem to 'whiten' the waves as an expression of fury; he shows how the
surge literally 'stood' before Achilles, and deluged him not just with
bloodstained water, but 'Blood'. The visual game he plays here, of 'now
you see the God, now you see the water', is the essence of the *Metamorphoses*. He is so confident of the treatment Homer needs in this episode
that he cuts two distracting elements of Hera's next speech (this is no
time for her to be referring to the fact that Vulcan is lame, or talking
about the pairing of the gods in Book XX), and plunges dramatically
in:

Fear touch'd the Queen of Heav'n: She saw dismay'd,
She call'd aloud, and summon'd *Vulcan's* Aid.
    Rise to the War! th'insulting Flood requires

Thy wasteful Arm: Assemble all thy Fires!
While to their aid, by our Command enjoin'd,
Rush the swift Eastern and the Western Wind:
These from old Ocean at my Word shall blow,
Pour the red Torrent on the wat'ry Foe,
Corses and Arms to one bright Ruin turn,
And hissing Rivers to their bottoms burn.
Go, mighty in thy Rage! display thy Pow'r,
Drink the whole Flood, the crackling Trees devour,
Scorch all the Banks! and (till our Voice reclaim)
Exert th'unweary'd Furies of the Flame!   (384–97)

The spirit of Ovid is coursing through Pope's pen to produce witty
ambiguities at each turn. Beneath 'th'insulting Flood' gleams the Latin
meaning of *insultare*, to leap; the red Torrent' Vulcan must pour is flame,
but he is to attack another torrent with it, which is also (Blood-) red.
The fire is to 'drink' a 'Flood' and 'devour crackling Trees': translation
here is unfettered creativity.

The Pow'r Ignipotent her Word obeys:
Wide o'er the Plain he pours the boundless Blaze;
At once consumes the dead, and dries the Soil;
And the shrunk Waters in their Chanel boil:
As when Autumnal *Boreas* sweeps the Sky,
And instant, blows the water'd Gardens dry:
So look'd the Field, so whiten'd was the Ground,
While *Vulcan* breath'd the fiery Blast around.
Swift on the sedgy Reeds the Ruin preys;
Along the Margin winds the running Blaze:
The Trees in flaming rows to Ashes turn,
The flow'ry *Lotos*, and the Tam'risk burn,
Broad Elm, and Cypress rising in a Spire;
The wat'ry Willows hiss before the Fire.
Now glow the Waves, the Fishes pant for Breath,
The Eels lie twisting in the Pangs of Death:
Now flounce aloft, now dive the scaly Fry,
Or gasping, turn their Bellies to the Sky.   (398–415)

In this fanciful vein Pope coins a new epithet for Vulcan, 'Ignipotent'
(by analogy with 'omnipotent' – Virgil calls Vulcan 'Ignipotens', *Aen.*
Vlll 414). As the fire takes a grip and scorches the plain we find the
first of several indications that Pope has in mind Ovid's description of
the burning of the earth by Phaeton (*Met.* II 210 ff.). This episode is

itself partly imitated from Homer, as we have noted; Ovid says wittily that Xanthus is about to burn a second time (II 245). At the opening of that description the fields are said to turn white ('pabula canescunt', II 212), hence Pope's 'so look'd the Field, so whiten'd was the Ground' (404). Pope's visual imagination then takes a firm hand with Homer's list of all the plants that get burned along the river (the original mentions elms, willows, tamarisk, clover, rushes and galingale, in no particular order and without distinguishing epithets): the blaze runs along the reedy banks, consumes trees 'in flaming rows', devours in picturesque contrast the 'Broad' elm and 'Cypress rising in a Spire' and triumphs with a witty version of doom for the willows: 'The wat'ry Willows hiss before the Fire' (406–11). The episode continues with the suffering of the river itself:

> Now glow the Waves, the Fishes pant for Breath,
> The Eels lie twisting in the Pangs of Death:
> Now flounce aloft, now dive the scaly Fry,
> Or gasping, turn their Bellies to the Sky.
> At length the River rear'd his languid Head,
> And thus short-panting, to the God he said.
>   O *Vulcan*, oh! what Pow'r resists thy Might?
> I faint, I sink, unequal to the Fight –
> I yield – Let *Ilion* fall; if Fate decree –
> Ah – bend no more thy fiery Arms on me!
>   He ceas'd; wide Conflagration blazing round;
> The bubbling Waters yield a hissing Sound.   (412–23)

Homer's eels and fish 'leap this way and that' in the hot water, but Pope's 'pant' and 'twist' with Ovidian characterisation – suggestively like the dying dragon in Addison's translation of *Metamorphoses* Book III:

> Till spent with Toil, and lab'ring hard for Breath,
> He now lay twisting in the Pangs of Death.[13]

When the fish gasp and 'turn their Bellies to the Sky' they are doing exactly what Ovid's seals do in Book II:

> Corpora phocarum summo resupina profundo
> Exanimata natant.

13 *Ovid's Metamorphoses*, ed. Samuel Garth (London: 1717), p. 77.

[The dead bodies of seals float on the water, belly upward]
(*Met.*, II 267–8)

And when the river finally capitulates, he does not merely 'address'
Vulcan, as he does in Homer, but audibly expires, panting and suffering
from an unprecedented migraine. All these delightful touches in Pope
(416–21) derive from Ovid's picture of Mother Earth, who puts her
hand to her brow, distraught at the drying up of her oceans:

> sustulit oppressos collo tenus arida vultus
> opposuitque manum fronti magnoque tremore
> omnia concutiens paullum subsedit ed infra,
> quam solet esse, fuit sacraque ita voce locuta est.

> [Though parched by heat she heaved up her smothered face.
> Lifting her hand to shield her brow and causing earthquakes
> with her trembling, she shrank back and spoke in these broken
> tones.]   (II 275–8)

Ovid's Earth, however, though 'hot smoke is choking her' (283), runs
on for twenty lines. Pope doubtless agreed with Addison, who remarked
'I cannot but think she speaks too much in any reason for one in her
condition.'[14] His own speech is an evocative masterpiece of brevity;
indeed, he is proud enough to list it in his index to remarkable effects
of versification at the end of the volume (under 'Expressing in the
Sound the Thing describ'd' – 'Out of Breath'). The river's voice is as
broken as Mother Earth's should have been ('I faint, I sink . . . I yield
. . . Ah –') and it disappears in a hiss as it comes to the boil: 'He ceas'd;
wide Conflagration blazing round;/ The bubbling Waters yield a hissing
Sound.' (418–23)

Pope thought Book XXI represented an 'entirely different' challenge
from the battle scenes preceding it: 'There is no Book of the Poem that
has more force of Imagination, or in which the great and inexhausted
Invention of our Author is more powerfully exerted' (VIII 420). It is a
mark of how fully that emerges in translation that we read Pope's
version as if it were not translation at all, and recognise how many other
authors go into Pope's recipe (Milton, Virgil, Ovid) without feeling that
the work has ceased to be Homeric. If Pope's first duty has been to
Homer's 'Spirit and Fire', then he is truly dutiful.

The habits of reading and composition that made it possible to

---

14 *Works*, ed. Thomas Tickell (London: 1721), I, p. 236.

appreciate what Pope was doing in this translation lasted, as we have seen, until Boswell and Johnson; but by the time of Cowper, the demand is being heard for a new, blank verse translation, 'unfettered' by rhyme. Pope's creativity is now seen as infidelity ('he has sometimes altogether suppressed the sense of his author, and has not seldom intermingled his own ideas with it' says Cowper, disapprovingly) and Cowper's promise in his Preface of 1791 is that of true fidelity, which means non-intervention:

> The English reader is to be admonished, that the matter found in me, whether he like it or not, is found also in HOMER, and that the matter not found in me, how much soever he may admire it, is found only in Mr. Pope. I have omitted nothing; I have invented nothing.[15]

If we look at Cowper's Book I invocation we do indeed find something completely new:

> Achilles sing, O Goddess! Peleus' son;
> His wrath pernicious, who ten thousand woes
> Caused to Achaia's host, sent many a soul
> Illustrious into Ades premature,
> And Heroes gave (so stood the will of Jove)
> To dogs and to all ravening fowls a prey,
> When fierce dispute had separated once
> The noble Chief Achilles from the son
> Of Atreus, Agamemnon, King of men.   (1–9)

Cowper is aiming for simplicity, and closeness to the original. But even he must ventriloquise through ghosts, for language does not spring from nowhere, and the presiding ghost here is Milton, who gives Cowper his inversions ('wrath pernicious', 'soul illustrious', 'separated once') and his reliance on heroic names ('the noble Chief Achilles', 'Agamemnon, King of Men'). It is a Miltonic coercion of grammar, too, that produces 'his wrath pernicious, who', referring back to Achilles; and it is also Milton who gives Cowper authority for calling Hades 'Ades', as in *Paradise Lost* (II 964).

Diction aside, what can we say of this as an invocation? The original turns on wrath and carnage. In his commitment to fidelity, Cowper

---

15 *Works of William Cowper*, ed. Robert Southey (London: Chiswick Press, 1837), XI, pp. viii–ix.

specifies these, but he must refuse to do more: thus we have an indistinct sense of catastrophe ('ten thousand woes'), conveyed by weak verbs ('sent', 'gave', 'separated') and hindered by linguistic puzzles ('Ades', 'so *stood* the will of Jove'). There are no bodies here, just 'Heroes' given 'to dogs and to all ravening fowls a prey'. When we compare Pope's

> Whose Limbs unbury'd on the naked Shore
> Devouring Dogs and hungry Vultures tore, (I 5–6)

we seem in Cowper to view the action through a screen of timidity.

Pope's private view of the couplet verse he so excelled at was surprisingly detached, but he had quite practical doubts about blank verse in English. Joseph Spence records him remarking in the 1730s,

> I have nothing to say for rhyme, but that I doubt whether a poem can support itself without it, in our language; unless it be stiffened with such strange words, as are likely to destroy our language itself. – The high style, that is affected so much in blank verse, would not have been borne, even in Milton, had not his subject turned so much on strange out-of-the-world things as it does.[16]

Cowper's problem is clearly how to 'support' the verse above prose without the 'stiffening' of strange words and situations. In his struggle to be both simple and epic he uses a kind of Miltonic starch, as we have seen, and gives the outline of the Homeric meaning without entering into its life. Applied to Vulcan's fight with the river Xanthus in Book XXI this method produces oddly literal effects:

> As when a sprightly breeze
> Autumnal blowing from the North, at once
> Dries the new-water'd garden, gladdening him
> Who tills the soil, so was the champain dried;
> The dead consumed, against the River, next,
> He turn'd the fierceness of his glittering fires.
> Willows and tamarisks and elms he burn'd,
> Burn'd lotus, rushes, reeds; all plants and herbs
> That clothed profuse the margin of his flood.
> His eels and fishes, whether wont to dwell

---

16 *Anecdotes, Observations and Characters of Books and Men*, ed. S.W. Singer (London: Centaur Press, 1964), p. 130.

In gulfs beneath, or tumble in the stream,
All languish'd while the Artist of the skies
Breath'd on them; even Xanthus lost, himself,
All force, and, suppliant, Vulcan thus address'd.
  Oh Vulcan! none in heaven itself may cope
With thee. I yield to thy consuming fires.
Cease, cease. I reck not if Achilles drive
Her citizens, this moment, forth from Troy,
For what are war and war's concerns to me?
  So spake he scorch'd, and all his waters boil'd.   (405–24)

This is not an impossible style: it is rapid and intermittently vivid (indeed 'the fierceness of his glittering fires', for Homer's 'supernatural fire', is an attractive lapse into the poetic diction Cowper planned to avoid). But it carries along with it grammatical problems so basic that its virtues are hard to appreciate: there are three different agents in the first ten lines, the farmer, Vulcan and Xanthus, all referred to as 'he/him/his' without explanation; and Vulcan becomes 'the Artist of the skies' (416), just when he has metamorphosed into flame, and no reader wants to be reminded of his other skills (Cowper would say that he is being faithful to the original, *polymetios Hephaistos*, 'inventive Hephaistos'). Most basic of all, the anthropomorphic river is introduced in grammar so inverted as to rob him of any presence in the poem, and his language sounds like what it is, translated Greek:

        . . . even Xanthus lost, himself,
    All force, and, suppliant, Vulcan thus address'd.
      Oh Vulcan! none in heaven itself may cope
    With thee. I yield to thy consuming fires.   (417–20)

This is not Homer's 'great and inexhausted Invention' but a bathetic collapse.

  The paradox that emerges from such fidelity is that it raises as many problems as infidelity. For by refusing to add to the original ('I have omitted nothing; I have invented nothing'), the translator actually escapes his primary responsibility, to make his original intelligible. He writes as if the Greek were visible to us, as it is to him; he forgets that all that we see of Homer is what he 'brings across', *trans-lates*, to us. This comparison between Cowper's method and Pope's may serve to illuminate this central issue in translation of whatever kind; and it may also help justify the suggestion made at the beginning, that the heroic couplet was a unique solution to these difficulties. For Cowper's problem, in essence, is that he needs more help – more help in generating meaning and in ironing out idiosyncrasies ('Ades', 'Artist of the Skies'). In rejecting the couplet, he is also rejecting the generations of other translators who have worked over each other's style and modified each other's solutions. All the help available to him in blank verse is Milton's; and while that is very valuable (as Pope would be the first to say), it is not enough. It rapidly degenerates into Miltonic pastiche; and the underlying message, 'this *must* be epic, because it sounds like Milton', is tinged with despair, where the ability of the couplet idiom to invoke other voices was, at best, a mark of historical confidence.

What is so remarkable about the heroic couplet is that it had implicit in it the whole English experience of the classics, the experience Pope invoked with his quotation from Lucretius; and what is still more suggestive is that in this respect, it is closer than any other poetic form to Homer's hexameter. 'Homer' is, of course, our shorthand for the oral tradition of formulaic composition; we now understand that the *Iliad* and *Odyssey* themselves are 'happy combinations of heroic diction' made from many dialects and many periods, as they evolved on the tongues of many skilful bards. The artificiality of Augustan poetic diction was the accusation made against it by Wordsworth and Coleridge that has reverberated down to our own time; but in the light of the greatness of the works that were created by Homeric formulae, is it really an accusation? And can a single poet ever hope to triumph without the serial effort of many?

Translation as the Creation of Images or 'Excuse me, is This the Same Poem?'

ANDRÉ LEFEVERE

IT IS SAID OF Dao'an, the famous translator of Buddhist scriptures into Chinese, that he had no knowledge of the source languages in which those scriptures were written, or rather, the source languages from which they were translated, and that he arrived at his final translations by means of a comparative study of various Chinese versions of the same scriptures.

I, too, do not know the source language from which the poet So Dongpo has been translated, and I, too, am comparing various English language versions of the Chinese original. I, too, am trying to make a virtue out of necessity. I tried to put myself into the shoes of somebody who knows very little about all three, but becomes interested in Chinese poetry in general, and in So Dongpo in particular. My question then became: how many So Dongpos are there for him? (I shall be using 'him' throughout this paper, not because I want to slight any 'hers,' but because fate has seen to it that I am a 'he,' for better or worse.) And, even more important: what kinds of So Dongpos are there for him? In other words, what images of So Dongpo did different translators create at different times for different audiences?

I further assumed that my alter ego would not really want to read absolutely everything written by So Dongpo, which would be impossible in translation anyway, but that he would want to get an impression of what So Dongpo is like based on rather liberal selections in anthologies that are more or less easily accessible to him. I know the subterfuge is glaringly obvious: of course my alter ego doesn't want to read all of So Dongpo because, if he did, he would force me to reveal even more of my ignorance than I shall be doing anyway. But I think I may be forgiven for employing this subterfuge because of what it may reveal: the puzzling refractions of what are, after all, always the same texts and what they tell us, not about the problem of translating, because that is not the one I am able to discuss in this case, but about the problem of translation, by which I mean the effect translated texts have on the audiences that read them. It is precisely because I do not know the language of the originals that the refractions are so puzzling, which puts me in exactly the same position as most readers of translations: they, too, cannot read the originals. Common sense might suggest that is precisely why they read translations, but common sense is one thing and thinking about translation is another. I thought I would write this paper because it presented a rare opportunity to move the one a bit closer to the other.

Not too many anthologies of Chinese literature in general, or Chinese poetry in particular, which are currently available in US bookstores and libraries, present my alter ego with selections from the work of So Dongpo that might be called representative enough for my alter ego to form his own image of the poet's work. My alter ego came up with ten to fifteen poems as a rule of thumb. Based on that admittedly somewhat arbitrary criterion he came up with the following four anthologies, listed here in chronological order: Alan Ayling and Duncan Mackintosh's *A Collection of Chinese Lyrics*, published in 1967, and *A Further Collection of Chinese Lyrics and Other Poems*, published in 1970, Kenneth Rexroth's *One Hundred Poems from the Chinese*, published in 1971, Wu-chi Liu and Irving Yucheng Lo's *Sunflower Splendor*, published in 1975, Burton Watson's *The Columbia Book of Chinese Poetry*, published in 1984, and Yang Xianyi and Gladys Yang's *Poetry and Prose of the Tang and Song*, also published in 1984. Needless to say, I also told him not to go back before 1960. After all, we are writing an article together, not a book.

Yet how can I, in good conscience, hide behind the construct of the 'average reader,' since I constructed him for a definite purpose? How dishonest can you get? Not more dishonest than many colleagues in other fields of literary inquiry who have been working with 'implied' or even 'ideal' readers who suspiciously resemble their creators. In fact it is precisely here that I can turn my handicap into an advantage for the project I want to undertake: because I do not know Chinese I am considerably less of an 'ideal' reader than I could be, which is excellent as far as this project goes because it stands or falls with the fact that I do not want to be one.

I shall now be reporting on my alter ego's findings. To organize the argument, I have based it on categories that emerged from a reading of different translations of the most often anthologized So Dongpo poem. That poem is variously called 'Ode to the Red Cliff' (Ayling 121), 'The Red Cliff' (Rexroth 65–66) and 'Memories of the Past at Red Cliff' (Yang 255). It will come as no surprise, I am sure, that the first category that came to mind was that of titles. Are these really the same poems? The comparison of the three titles mentioned above is a relatively mild case, as I hope to show later, but already relatively confusing.

The second category is that of references made inside the poem to the world outside of it. The same lines (at least as far as my alter ego could make out) are rendered by Ayling as 'The western side of the old fort/ Was once, so people say,/ Known as the Red Cliff of Chou of the Three kingdoms', by Rexroth as 'To the West of the ancient/Wall you enter the Red Gorge/ Of Chu Ko liang of the/ Days of the Three Kingdoms', and by Yang as 'This ancient rampart on its Western shore/ Is Zhou Yu's Red Cliff of the Three Kingdoms' fame.' This, too, is rather puzzling, and footnotes do not always bring enlightenment. Ayling retells the whole story of what he calls the 'San Kuo Chih Yen I' (238), without telling his readers what the title means. Yet, by doing so, he manages to situate the characters that occur later on in So Dongpo's poem in such a way that the reader is able to understand why they are referred to in the following lines. Yang (I should really say 'the Yangs', just as I should say 'Ayling and Mackintosh', but I have opted for this kind of shorthand) is much more sparing with his footnotes. In fact he only gives one which must, of necessity, turn out to be more than a little cryptic in the light of the wealth of historical information contained in the poem. Yang's footnote reads: 'Scene of the Battle in A.D. 208 when Liu Bei and Sun Quan defeated Cao Cao's advancing forces' (255). Beyond all the vagaries of different systems of transliteration my alter ego, like all other readers of Chinese poetry in translation, learned to take in his stride, his confusion was heightened by the fact that the 'Liu Bei' and the 'Sun Quan' Yang refers to are conspicuously absent from the long footnote provided by Ayling. Of course different names may refer to the same people, but my alter ego has no way of knowing this. Rexroth, in contrast, does not give any footnotes at all, leaving my alter ego, again in the company of all readers of Chinese poetry in translation, to wonder who Kung Ch'in, Chiao-siao, Chu Ko Liang, and Ts'ao Ts'ao might be, especially since Kung Ch'in appears to be 'Marshal Zhou Yu' in Yang's translation, in which Chiao-siao seems to be referred to as 'the Lord Qiao's younger daughter' and from which Chu Ko Liang and Ts'ao Ts'ao have (mysteriously?) disappeared, as they also have from Ayling's translation.

The third category is that of style and diction. Compare the following lines that all purport to render the same original. Ayling has 'With piled up rocks to stab the sky/ And waves to shake them thunderously/ Churning the frothy mass to mounds of snow/ It's like a masterpiece in paint./ Those ages hide how many a hero.' Rexroth renders the (presumably) same lines as 'The/ Jagged peaks pierce the heavens./ The furious rapids beat/ At the boat, and dash up in/ A thousand clouds of spray like/ Snow. Mountain and river have/ Often been painted, in the/ Memory of the heroes/ Of those days.' Finally, Yang writes: 'Here jagged boulders pound the clouds,/ Huge waves tear banks apart,/ And foam piles up a thousand drifts of snow;/ A scene fair as a painting,/ Countless the brave men here in time gone by!'

Apart from some inconsistencies, such as Yang's 'boulders pounding' the skies and Ayling's 'rocks stabbing' them, whereas Rexroth's 'peaks pierce' them, my alter ego was puzzled the most by what happened to the painting in the translations. From Ayling and Yang he got the impression that So Dongpo is saying that the scene he has just described is worthy of a painting, which is hardly surprising because he created such paintings himself. From Rexroth, on the other hand, he got the impression that many paintings of the scene have, indeed, been painted, and that they have been painted specifically to commemorate the heroes who fell in the battle.

There seems to be a rather grave inconsistency here, but of what nature? Is my alter ego faced with a mere logical inconsistency, did Rexroth get it wrong, or what? Perhaps the explanation can be found more readily in the realm of poetics. Rexroth is bent on writing a poem that is more narrative than evocative, and certainly one that has to make narrative sense. There can be no missing links, which is why the paintings not only have to be real, and many, but they also have to have been painted in memory of the heroes. Add to this that Rexroth uses a basic three foot line, and you get a much more streamlined version of the original, one that reads indeed like an American poem of its time, perhaps one loosely affiliated with the style of the Black Mountain poets, particularly Robert Creeley, whose longer poems display the same inclination to use the run-on line more often than not. What I am suggesting (and what my alter ego, along with many readers of Chinese poetry in translation could probably put into these same words) is that the poetics more or less dominant in the receiving literature at the time a translation is made is probably the most fundamental choice the translator makes. It is because Rexroth wanted to produce the kind of poem I briefly described above that he did actually produce it, subordinating other considerations, such as the presence/absence of logical links and rhyme, to the model of the poem he had in his mind.

Ayling tries to use rhyme as often as possible, not least since rhyme is used in the original anyway. The price to be paid is a somewhat erratic line length and a compulsion to rhyme, wherever possible, which tends to subvert the syntax of the translation at times, as in the line 'Those ages hide how many a hero!' which appears to have the form it has because it has to rhyme with 'snow' two lines up. Ayling tends to use a variable line in the tradition of the Florence Ayscough translations. Whereas the variable line may be traced to Hopkins's metrical experiments in English poetry, it is doubtful, at least to my mind, that Ayling would have been consciously emulating Hopkins. Rather, another mechanism in the practice of translation may well have become operative here: that of the tradition. Ayling is translating the way he is because Ayscough has been translating like that before him, just as Yang is translating in a certain way because Waley did so before. There is, in other words, a 'translation poetics' just as there is a poetics that helps guide the development and production of original literature. One type of Chinese translation poetics has been well described by John Smith in his foreword to Ayling's second anthology, where he states that Ayling's collection 'destroys the comfortable myth that Chinese poetry was written in a sort of Lawrentian free verse, was of a permanently dying cadence and enervatingly nostalgic' (*Further Lyrics* x). The two poetics do not overlap, which would explain the survival, in Yang's translations, of the kind of diction that was current in Waley's time. Yang's 'A scene fair as a painting' appears to me to be a case in point, even apart from, or perhaps exactly because the 'fair' in that line hardly corresponds to the description of the boulders, the waves, and the foam. The 'fair' appears to be a case of diction running on empty, an example of a type of translation poetics generating its own clichés. The same type of cliché is, again to my mind, present in Ayling's line 'Churning the frothy mass to mounds of snow', also quoted above.

For Rexroth, on the other hand, there is no doubt that Chinese poetry will only be read and enjoyed by readers who know English and no Chinese if the translator is successful in making it conform completely to what those readers expect an English language poem of their time to be like. Ayling, on the other hand, wants it understood that the poetry he is translating is written according to a poetics that is not that of the receiving literature. In fact, he constantly reminds his readers of this by having his books published as facing page editions. Even for the reader who knows no Chinese at all, and therefore has no way of checking the translations, the presence of Chinese characters, and the occasional reproduction of a Chinese painting on the page facing each actual translation, serve as a reminder of the fact that what he is reading cannot really be read according to the poetics of his own literature. The problem, of course, is that translators usually do not tell him what the poetics of the original are, thus often leaving both their translations and their readers in a state of limbo.

Watson and Liu and Lo try to give their readers a good idea of what Chinese poetics is like by means of longish introductions preceding their actual translations, and also by means of footnotes, which tend to be more extensive in Liu and Lo than in Watson. Liu and Lo print a translation entitled 'At the Heng-ts'ui Pavilion of Fa-hui Monastery', which corresponds to Yang's 'The Pavilion of Green Hills in Fahui Temple'. Liu and Lo explain the Heng-ts'ui in the title as follows: 'Heng-ts'ui (literally 'kingfisher recumbent'), a name given to this pavilion, refers to the mountains in front of it. This phrase is also a poetic epithet referring to a woman's eyebrows; the fashion at that time was to paint them green' (342). Obviously, the footnote helps the readers (my alter ego among them) not only to situate the title of the poem, but also to understand the allusive way in which So Dongpo's poetry operates. Yang's 'Green Hills' does nothing of the kind. Similarly, Liu and Lo explain the Wu Mountain's 'tossing and turning to look its best for you' by means of the following footnote:

> This line contains two allusions. First, the words 'toss' (*chuan*) and 'turn' (*ts'e*) come from the first poem in the *Shih Ching*, generally interpreted as an epithalamium ode. The comparison of the mountain to a woman is reinforced by the second allusion: *wei chün jung*, the last three words of the line (literally: 'to wear makeup for you'), a common idiom describing a wife's duty (342–43).

Yang does not give any footnote at all, leaving the reader at a loss to appreciate not only the deeper layers of meaning in the original, but also the poet's consummate artistry.

Yang prints a poem entitled 'A Poem' (238–39), which corresponds to Watson's 'The New Year's Eve Blizzard' (301–02). Watson's translation is preceded by the following introduction: 'Written in 1077 when the poet was on his way from Mi-chou to the capital before proceeding to his next post as governor of Hsü-chou. 5-ch. old style.' The reader can make sense of the last sentence of this introduction because Watson has taken great pains to explain the whole generic system of T'ang and Sung poetry in the general introduction to his anthology, as indeed have Liu and Lo. Doing so also gives both anthologies a kind of dispensation from rhyming, precisely the dispensation Ayling cannot claim because he does not give the reader an idea of what the original was 'really' like. Yang usually identifies the genre or type of poem, but does not tell the reader where it fits into the greater generic scheme. Rexroth does not bother with Chinese poetics at all, having opted for a translation that should put the (Western) poetics of the receiving culture first.

When comparing Yang's and Watson's translations of this poem, the reader is immediately struck by the difference in diction. Perhaps the most obvious illustration of that difference is to be found in Yang's fourth line, which also corresponds to Watson's fourth line. Yang writes: 'As I jog along on my lean nag, half dreaming still'. Watson has: 'On a lean horse, I nod in the remains of a dream.' No doubt like many English-language readers who have been familiarized with the poetry written in that language, my alter ego experienced a strong preference for Watson's translation. The preference is of course based 'merely' on the fact that Watson's diction is also that of contemporary English language poetry, whereas Yang's translation is rejected because nobody says 'nag' any more, and 'jog' has acquired connotations in present-day English, especially American English, that make the line, as it stands, come perilously close to the grotesque.

There is another important point here, namely that no diction can spoil an image, as long as that image is transposed directly. Compare Watson's 'Flakes big as goose feathers hang from the horse's mane/ till I think I'm riding a great white bird' (302) to Yang's 'Flakes cling like goose feathers to my horse's mane,/ And I marvel to find myself riding a white phoenix' (238). The image comes across well in both translations, but Yang's diction veers off into the overly discursive in the next line. This is, ultimately, again a matter of translation poetics. Waley may well be behind the line in question, but I think another line of the same poem, translated by Yang as 'Why complain, then, of the hardships of the journey?' (239) which corresponds to Watson's 'Do I grumble at the trials of official travel?' (302), can claim an ancestry that may well stretch back all the way to Legge and Giles.

The problem of diction is compounded somewhat by the fact that Chinese scholars have, in the past, dauntlessly translated their literature into English and, to a lesser extent, other Western languages. They figure prominently among the relatively few instances of translation with artistic pretensions from the mother tongue into a foreign language. This translational attitude is no doubt inspired by a great reverence for the native tradition and a concomitant desire to make that tradition known abroad. In practice, though, it tends to reinforce translation poetics which, as I suggested above, always lags somewhat behind the current dominant poetics in the receiving culture, at the expense of that poetics, a fact which renders the reception of the translations more difficult.

In the lines clustered around the image of the goose feathers quoted above, Yang's So Dongpo is riding a phoenix, whereas Watson's So Dongpo is simply riding a great white bird. Like most readers, my alter ego is at a loss as to who is riding what. Probably a phoenix, but if so, why doesn't Yang explain in a footnote what a phoenix is? Probably because he did not think it necessary. On the other hand, the big white bird might simply be a big white bird. Or it could be that Watson has opted for a big white bird because he can then deftly sidestep the problem of the footnote: you don't have to explain what you don't mention. We are faced here with the problem of progressive acculturation. Chinese poetry (and literature in general) have been translated often enough; there are enough Chinatowns and Amy Tans and Timothy Mos for an image of China to have established itself in the mind of the Western reader. Certain elements of that image – and they are usually the most mundane ones, since acculturation tends to take place primarily through the stomach in a first phase – such as chop suey do not need a footnote any more. Other elements of the culture might already have reached that level of acculturation, but then again, they might not, and it is up to the respective translators to decide the point at which a footnote changes from a help to understanding to an insult to the reader's intelligence. This problem is compounded by the fact that the translator, with the exception here of Rexroth, is a specialist, who doesn't really know what the 'common' reader knows and does not know.

The problem of progressive acculturation is not just limited to lines; it can, and does, spill over into whole poems. Compare the following short poem, called 'Crab Apple' by Yang (245) and 'Begonias' by Rexroth (86). First Yang:

> In the spring breeze a blaze of flaming brightness,
> A fragrant mist as the moon rounds the covered walk;
> Afraid the flowers may fall asleep at night,
> I light tall candles to shine on that crimson glory.

Then Rexroth:

> The East wind blows gently.
> The rising rays float
> On the thick perfumed mist.
> The moon appears, right there,
> At the corner of the balcony.
> I only fear in the depth of night

The flowers will fall asleep.
I hold up a gilded candle
To shine on their scarlet beauty.

Part of my alter ego is inclined to think that this is, indeed, the same poem, whereas the other part remains somewhat sceptical about that conclusion. The point, though, is that he'll never know unless someone tells him, and he should not need anyone to tell him. The problem appears to be Rexroth's insistence of some kind of local color, on the 'scene' of China he has in his head and 'frames' accordingly in his translation, whether it is there in the original or not. Rexroth's scene of China seems to involve the East wind, which may just be Yang's spring breeze, and that East wind has to 'blow gently', whereas in Yang it is just there. Rexroth's 'rising rays' are somewhat reminiscent of the rising sun associated with the East by many Westerners, and the mist has to be 'perfumed' in his poem because perfume is another part of his Chinese scene. His 'rising rays' are somewhat weaker than Yang's 'flaming brightness', but then again that 'flaming brightness' might have appeared in the line because of assonance and alliteration: the 'brightness' would then pair off nicely with the 'breeze' and the 'blaze', whereas the 'flaming' assonates again with the 'blaze' and is picked up by the 'fragrant' in the next line.

Confusion is heightened by the fact that Rexroth, having sovereignly decided to give absolute priority to Western poetics, does not try to keep the form of the original at all. As a result, his lines are shorter and more in number: three to Yang's first line. Yang's second line again pays tribute to a certain translation poetics: 'the moon rounds the covered walk', whereas Rexroth's fourth and fifth lines are in keeping with the emphasis on concreteness dominant in the poetics of his time. That emphasis explains why the moon has to be 'right there' and why the 'covered walk' is Californianized into a 'balcony'. It is interesting, and frustrating, to note here that my alter ego has no clue what the original refers to. Is the 'covered walk' something you find around the courtyards of Western medieval castles, and especially monasteries? And surely the balcony cannot be what he looks out from every day at the swimming pool under it?

Suddenly Yang's third line matches almost completely with Rexroth's sixth and seventh lines, which may mean my more optimistic alter ego is right and we are dealing with the same original poem indeed. Some doubts are sown again by the fact that Yang's 'tall candles' seem to have become one 'gilded candle' in Rexroth, but again, my alter ego knows a little about Chinese grammar not to be too upset by such details, and he puts the difference between 'crimson glory' in Yang and 'scarlet beauty' in Rexroth down to poetics, translation poetics in the first case, the dominant poetics of Rexroth's time in the second. But still, my alter ego will never really know for sure.

Titles, as suggested above, create by far the worst confusion. How is my alter ego to know, for instance, that what Yang calls 'The Moon Festival' (251–52) corresponds to Liu and Lo's 'Prelude to Water Music' (350), that Rexroth's 'A Walk in the Country' (76) corresponds to Watson's 'Rhyming with Tzu-yu's "Treading the Green" ' (297), and that Rexroth's 'Autumn' (88) corresponds to Watson's 'Presented to Liu Ching-wen' (308). Needless to say, these examples are more than just mildly amusing: they have to do with the solutions various translators try to find to the problem of the radically different poetics they work with.

But what of the image of So Dongpo my alter ego gets from the selections in the different anthologies, because that was the original object of the exercise? The biographical notes in the various anthologies are interesting in this respect. Rexroth gives nothing on So Dongpo at all, leaving my alter ego to guess what Yang tells him straight away, namely that So Dongpo was not just 'the leading poet of the Northern Song period' (227), but also 'a celebrated calligrapher and painter' (227). Yang gives So Dongpo bad marks because 'he often took a conservative political stand' (227), but praises him because 'he often played a more progressive role in the world of letters by opposing the formalism then dominant' (227), only to round off his short introduction with the most amazing strings of clichés: 'His poetry is fresh and original and his prose is distinguished by its vividness, rich in imagery and boldness of vision' (227). Yang's classifying of So Dongpo as conservative in politics conflicts somewhat with Liu and Lo's description of him as having suffered reversals in his career partly due to the 'acerbity of his writing' (589). Watson goes even further than this, stating that So Dongpo was known for his 'sharp criticism of government policy, some of it expressed in his poems' (296). The reader has little alternative but to think that the government of So Dongpo's time must have been very enlightened and progressive indeed. It is further significant that although Yang's anthology deals with both the Tang and Song periods, So Dongpo gets 36 poems, as opposed to 26 for Du Fu and only 20 for Li Bai. Half of Rexroth's anthology is devoted to Tu Fu, the other half only to Sung poets because, in Rexroth's opinion, 'the whole spirit of this time is very congenial today, especially to the romantic, empirical-mystic, and antinomian taste which has prevailed in the arts of the West since 1940' (xii). He gives So Dongpo 25 poems, far more than any other poet except Tu Fu.

Liu and Lo round out the picture of So Dongpo a bit more, by informing the reader that So Dongpo 'achieved pre-eminence in many fields which included *shih*, *tz'u*, belletristic prose, as well as calligraphy and painting' (589). In their general introduction Liu and Lo proceed, as stated above, to give a survey of the different genres of Chinese poetry, which allows the reader to evaluate So Dongpo's versatility and craftsmanship. Yang also states that 'as well as *shi*, the classical verse form, he also wrote *ci* poetry to melodies dating from the 8th Century' (227), but without explaining the difference between shi and ci, and without informing the reader of the role played by music in the ci as a genre.

Where Liu and Lo state that So Dongpo was born 'into a family of modest means' (589), Yang lets him be born into 'a family with a long tradition of government service' (227), whereas Ayling lets him be born into 'a very talented family' (111). Liu and Lo also point out that So Dongpo's 'father and the two sons all became outstanding prose writers and poets' (589), making it easy for the reader to understand why so many of So Dongpo's poems are written in reply or reaction to poems written by his brother. In marked contrast to Yang's platitudes quoted above, Liu and Lo conclude their portrayal of So Dongpo with a statement that allows the reader to grasp why he is such an important figure, particularly in the development of the tz'u: 'his achievement as a tz'u writer is considered extraordinary in that he has accommodated lyric poetry to all kinds of themes and broadened its scope' (590). They give 17 poems to So Dongpo, as opposed to 18 to Li Po and 32 to Tu Fu.

Watson gives 22 poems to So Dongpo, 19 to Li Po, and 18 to Du Fu, which seems to confirm the impression that So Dongpo's star is on the rise in the eighties. Considering the fact that Ayling's two anthologies only contain tz'u poems, one would expect So Dongpo to figure prominently in both of them. He only gets six poems in the first anthology, but 'about a third of the lyrics in our new book [*Further Lyrics*] is the work of Su Shih and of Hsin Ch'i-chi' (*Further Lyrics* xiii). In other words, one sixth of the 'new book' is devoted to So Dongpo. As already stated above, Ayling is also the only one to explain why Su Shi is also called 'Su Tung P'o', an obvious illustration of the 'specialist syndrome' mentioned earlier: since sinologists know that Su Shih is also So Dongpo, the common reader is also supposed to know. Instead, the common reader is told by Ayling that: 'Su Shih called himself the Recluse of the Eastern Slope (Tung P'o)' (111).

Judging from the poems that have been selected in the various anthologies, Rexroth's So Dongpo is a poet who writes about transience and the need to enjoy life before it is too late (six poems), who produces nature descriptions (six poems), and who writes the odd poem about sorrow, resignation, serenity, happiness. Rexroth's So Dongpo is mainly a nature poet aware of the transience of life.

Yang's So Dongpo adds one important dimension left out completely in Rexroth, even though Rexroth translated six of So Dongpo's poems that have nature as their subject matter. We have to wait until we see titles like 'Written on a Painting of Autumn Scenery by Li Shinan' (246) and 'Monk Huichong's Painting 'Dusk on the Spring River'' (246) until we are able to realize that the fact that So Dongpo was also a calligrapher and a painter did indeed influence his output as a poet. The other category Yang adds to our impression of So Dongpo's work is, not surprisingly, that of socially committed poetry in poems like 'A Lament for Lichees' (247–48), 'A Poem' (238), and 'Lament of a Peasant Woman' (233), presumably all written at moments when So Dongpo did not feel excessively conservative. Yet another category is that of poems written about and dedicated to his brother, often dealing with reminiscence and separation. Still another category is that of the religious poem, and the poet as a public official is revealed in two poems written about exile. All in all, Yang's So Dongpo writes ten nature poems, four poems about his brother, five poems about transience, among them one on the death of his wife, four poems with social content, four religious poems, two poems observing people, two poems on exile, two riddles, and one poem celebrating happiness.

Liu and Lo add the category of animal poems and expand that of observations of human beings. Their So Dongpo writes only four nature poems, four poems about people, four poems about transience, four religious poems, two poems about exile, and one poem about politics. He is much more of a balanced all-round poet, which of course highlights, if that was still necessary, the enormous real power translators and anthologists wield in constructing the image of writers for those who cannot read their work in the original.

Watson widens So Dongpo's reach even more by including a poem about children and friends. He includes only one poem about transience, two about the poet's brother, four social poems, only two nature poems, only one religious poem, two poems about exile, and two poems about happiness.

Finally, Ayling's So Dongpo writes seven poems about transience and six poems about nature. Most of the other subjects mentioned above get one poem each. It should be remembered, of course, that Ayling's anthology was published first, chronologically, so that the other anthologies may also be seen as attempts to correct the So Dongpo found in that anthology. Still, and this again goes a long way towards establishing the principle of the power of tradition in translation, eleven of the poems selected and translated by Ayling also appear in one or more of the other anthologies. Ayling may therefore be said to have begun a 'secondary canonization', or canonization in translation, if you will, of So Dongpo.

We have now established which So Dongpo, or So Dongpos, are available in translation to my alter ego and other readers of his ilk. We have also learned something about translation in the process. It remains to summarize briefly what. The most obvious lesson we have learned is, to my mind, that translation, though it obviously has quite a bit to do with language and, as I have argued at great length elsewhere, with power, is in this case mostly a matter of comparative poetics. It is also obvious why that lesson is so obvious. Before we say goodbye to my alter ego we would do well to remember that he is utterly unfamiliar with Chinese poetics and that he, and other readers of his ilk, would not have been as confused if they had been faced with translations from another Western language. The language would have been different, of course, but the poetics would have been more than recognizable. In this case, though, my alter ego is faced with the unknown. Not only does he not know how to read the language, he also does not know how to read the translated text, where it fits into its culture and what its relationship is with other texts of the same and, especially, different kinds.

Perhaps humankind's most immediate and predictable reaction to the unknown is that of analogy. The only way we can conceptualize what we do not know is to liken it to something we do know, and extrapolate from there.

The problem is the unknown; the reaction is analogy, but is it also the solution? I think not, because analogy, especially if based on a certain power structure, tends unfortunately to exhibit a certain unmistakable pull towards arrogance. And the first victim of the arrogance of analogy is precisely what is most particular to the original, the very feature in which the original is most itself: its form. In terms of the So Dongpo translations under analysis here, the arrogance of analogy most obviously reveals itself in the Kenneth Rexroth translations,

particularly in the title of one of them: 'Epigram' (84). The title reveals
Rexroth's decision, already alluded to earlier, to give absolute priority
to the poetics dominant in the receiving culture.

Analogy is often defended on the grounds that it is necessary to give
the receiving audience something they recognize if one wants to make
sure they are actually going to 'receive' it or, in other words, that it is
actually going to make an impact on the receiving culture. This is
obviously the strategy employed by Rexroth who hopes that his translations will be 'true to the spirit of the original and valid English poems'
(xi). The problem is whether the latter does not make the former
impossible, especially if one knows that Rexroth, by his own admission,
'usually translated from other Western languages, mostly the French of
Soulié de Morant and G. Margouliès' (xi). No wonder sinologists like
Liu and Lo inveigh against this practice, which is usually supplemented
by what they call the 'use of informants, which was often resorted to
by missionaries and amateurs even in the not so distant past' (x). That
past is four years earlier in Rexroth's case, and the informants he used
will have been friends and students. His translations appear to owe
much to the institution that attempted to regulate the first intrusion
of translation into the citadel of US academe: the translation workshop,
where empathy, rather than knowledge of languages, usually led to the
creation of usually utterly analogous translations, so utterly analogous,
in fact, that they all resembled the works written by the published writer
who usually led the workshop, no matter who their graduate student
authors were.

If Rexroth is the one extreme, it is doubtful whether Liu and Lo's
utopian call for

> accuracy as well as readability. The translation aims at preserving, in
> idiomatic English, the identity of the original, including most of its
> grammatical and stylistic features (parts of speech, word order, line
> length and enjambment, the use of parallelism, and sometimes even
> auditory devices); however, no attempt has been made to reproduce
> the rhyme scheme. (x)

One's first reaction, unfair though it may seem, is of course: why not?
Why not try to reproduce the rhyme scheme if you are trying to
reproduce all the rest anyway, as if reproducing all the rest was not
difficult enough?

As opposed to this 'almost all or almost nothing' approach, which is
also advocated by Ayling, who states that 'the object has been to reflect,

as far as possible, the meaning, 'shape' (differing lengths and strengths of lines) and ornamentation of each lyric, in English verse, that seeks to keep the Chinese spirit' (xiii), Watson pleads for compromise, observing that

> classical Chinese poetry was only successfully translated into English when the translators were willing to set aside the rhymes and meters of traditional English verse, as well as Western concepts of what constitutes poetic diction and subject matter, and create a freer form that would permit the power and expressiveness of the originals to shine through. (*Lyrics* 13)

But then again, the question is how do they shine through as Chinese originals, how can the translator make sure they are not just perceived as free verse? Nothing against free verse as such, of course, except that in many, if not all cases, it serves to obscure rather than reveal the consummate craftsmanship of poets writing heavily regulated *shih* and *tz'u* style poems.

If readers like my alter ego are ever going to be really exposed to Chinese poetry, they need to be exposed to its form as well as its content. Ayling, Liu and Lo, and Watson are not to blame: the first two try their best to reproduce as many features of the original as they can, Ayling even to the point of including the occasional rhyme. Watson opts for a different strategy, but at least he tells his readers as much as possible about the form he has not been able to reproduce, hoping that the information given will somehow 'jell' inside the reader's head with the actual translations offered.

This may well be the best we can hope for, at least for the time being. Liu and Lo's anthology sometimes comes close to what has been advocated in recent years as 'resistive' translation, the kind of translation that would translate the original in such a way that its salient features would be immediately recognizable in the translation, transforming that translation, in fact, into a text that is situated in a no man's land between two literatures/cultures, and as such forces the reader to come to terms with the original nature of the original.

I cannot provide any solutions, and that is not my task, and not just because I am incapable of doing so in this case because I do not know Chinese. I firmly believe that I (or anyone else, for that matter) should not offer solutions, because solutions imposed tend to harden into yet another kind of translation poetics. Rather, what I have tried to do is to show how existing translations really affect readers of which my alter ego is but poor representative. Yet they are tremendously important in the world of translation: if readers do not 'receive' translations in any meaningful way, the originals of those translations will not enter into the culture of those readers, no matter how good the translators' intentions are. Their intentions are not in doubt, nor is their creativity. If we ever are to study literature beyond national boundaries, in a way that respects each constituent literature's distinctive features, we have to encourage our translators to experiment with solutions to the problems I have tried to outline above.

Works Cited

Ayling, Alan, and Duncan Mackintosh. *A Collection of Chinese Lyrics*. Nashville: Vanderbilt University Press, 1967.

Ayling, Alan, and Duncan Mackintosh. *A Further Collection of Chinese Lyrics*. Nashville: Vanderbilt University Press, 1970.

Liu, Wu-chi, and Irving Yucheng Lo, eds. *Sunflower Splendor*. Garden City, New York: Anchor Books, 1975.

Rexroth, Kenneth. *One Hundred Poems from the Chinese*. New York: New Directions, 1971.

Watson, Burton, ed. and translator. *The Columbia Book of Chinese Poetry*. New York: Columbia University Press, 1984.

Yang, Xianji, and Gladys Yang. *Poetry and Prose of the Tang and Song*. Beijing: Panda Books, 1984.

Translation and National Canons:
Slav perceptions of English romanticism

PIOTR KUHIWCZAK

Farewell, my Russia, sad and sordid!
To slaves and masters my adieu.
Farewell, blue uniforms – and lord it
Over the men that cringe to you.

Who knows? Perhaps 'mid brave Caucasians
I'll hide myself from your viziers,
From searching eyes on all occasions,
From ever-present, open ears.[1]

IT IS PRESUMED THAT THE Russian poet Mikhail Lermontov wrote this poem in 1841, just before being sent into exile. For obvious political reasons, the poem could not be published during the poet's lifetime, and the Russian text – which appeared as late as 1887 – is not based on any manuscript, but on the record of someone claiming to have heard the poem from Lermontov's own mouth.

The poem is essentially just what we would expect of a typical Russian or East European Romantic poem. The poetic voice is that of a political rebel who is forced to go into exile, but just hours before his departure manages to write an intense denunciation of oppressive power. The misty origins of the text are easily interpreted as the best proof that the poem was based on a spontaneous and authentic impulse, and the printed versions, which appeared long after Lermontov's death, may be read as genuine records of oral transmission. But if the origins of this poem can be called 'Ossianic', anyone candidly examining its form and contents might well conclude that they are inherently Byronic. A close textual affinity of this poem to any of Byron's poems would be difficult to prove, but one cannot ignore the fact that the English poet had cornered the market, as it were – not just at home, but abroad – in writing lyrics about parting with people and places.

---

[1] M. Lermontov, *Major Poetical Works*, trans. A. Liberman (London, 1983), lines 1–8.

The best-known 'parting' of all comes from the first canto of *Childe Harold's Pilgrimage*:

> Adieu, adieu! my native shore
>   Fades o'er the waters blue;
> The night-winds sigh, the breakers roar,
>   And shrieks the the wild sea-mew.
> Yon sun that sets upon the sea
>   We follow in his flight;
> Farewell awhile to him and thee,
>   My native Land – Good Night!
>
> A few short hours, and he will rise
>   To give the morrow birth;
> And I shall hail the main and skies,
>   But not my mother earth.
> Deserted is my own good hall,
>   Its hearth is desolate;
> Wild weeds are gathering on the wall,
>   My dog howls at the gate.[2]

Childe Harold's reasons for leaving home and Byron's for turning his back on England were actually less compelling than Lermontov's. A desolate hall, weeds and a howling dog are well known signs of Romanticism – they evoke deep melancholy, whenever the desired mood is needed. Lermontov, like many other East European poets, did not have to look for artificial means to represent his feelings and predicament. The stark reality was omnipresent and it could be transformed into a literary text without the use of highly conventionalized phrases. The blue uniforms of which Lermontov writes were those of Tsarist soldiers, and under an absolute monarchy the country was indeed sad and sordid. Spies were watching and listening to every word and recording every independent act and gesture. But in Byron's case the circumstantial details were not that important, either for the poet or his European readers. What mattered much more was the fact that his poetry bore a stamp of 'authenticity' – that the moment of artistic creation seemed to be triggered by an actual event. Life and art were deliberately enmeshed together by the poet – to the point where even he was unable to disentangle them.

---

[2] Lord Byron, *Childe Harold's Pilgrimage*, ed. J. McGann (Oxford, 1980), canto 1, stanza XIII.

Lermontov was an avid reader of Byron's poetry, in French translation. He also read all the accounts of Byron's life he could lay his
hands on, as well as Byron's letters, and never bothered to conceal how
deeply he was inspired by both the life and writings of the English poet.
However, unlike many lesser European Byronists, he clearly knew the
difference between genuine literary borrowing and a fashionable social
pose. In fact, the difference between himself and Byron became the
theme of one of his better-known lyrics:

> No, I am not Byron, though I and he
> Were both exposed to fame and danger;
> 'Mid men a wanderer and stranger,
> I have a Russian soul in me.
> I started young, I'll finish sooner,
> My soul is like a shipwrecked schooner
> That sank with all its broken hopes.[3]

Lermontov's case is just one instance of what is generally known as
'European Byronism'. The phenomenon is well-documented and has
been extensively analysed.[4] There is general agreement among critics
that Byronism was a literary and cultural phenomenon arising from the
specific political context of early nineteenth-century Europe. Since
then perceptions of English Romanticism have changed focus, and no
modern critic would insist that Byronism was the most important
literary phenomenon of that period. Eastern Europe itself sees things
differently. Good translations of Keats, Shelley and Wordsworth have
been made available in Russian, Czech and Polish, and it is well-known
that the English have never had much time or patience for Byron's
poetry after the initial euphoria. However, it is debatable whether this
shift of critical perspective has radically altered the ordinary reader's
canon of English Romantics outside Britain. If Byron has fewer readers
today than ever before, it does not mean that other English romantics
have gained more popularity. When asked about English literature, any
literate Pole would name Shakespeare and Byron as its main figures,
and the same view would probably prevail amongst Czechs and Russians
too. This is in spite of the fact that the social and literary scene in
Eastern Europe has recently undergone a seismic upheaval, and East

---

[3] M. Lermontov, *Major Poetical Works*, lines 1–7.
[4] See, for instance, *Byron's Political and Cultural Influence in Nineteenth
Century Europe*, ed. P.G. Trueblood (London, 1981).

Europeans now cherish more down-to-earth literary characters than Byron's noble fighters for freedom. In the early 1980s it is true that heroic lines translated from *The Age of Bronze* were used as graffiti in Gdansk, but today such an application for a literary text in Poland would be inconceivable.

The reason why Byron is still second only to Shakespeare in the East European version of the canon probably has nothing to do with current taste or politics. Byron's unassailable position was established long ago, by the nineteenth-century translators, writers and critics who turned him into an East European Romantic. As a result, Byron became a part of the various East European national canons in much the same way that the great Russian writers of the last century were domesticated in Britain. If the translation of any literary text is to leave a mark on the receiving culture, it must aim beyond what is normally understood as linguistic equivalence. Translation theorists would say that in order to gain real standing a foreign text must be either entirely 'domesticated' – i.e. must create the impression that it is not a translation but written in the original language – or break the literary rules of the receiving culture to such an extent that it acquires the status of an artistic innovation.[5] The literary history of many countries supplies us with suggestive examples. Pope domesticated *The Iliad*, Schlegel and his followers turned Shakespeare into a German poet, and Chekhov has been assimilated into the repertoire of English theatre. At the other end of the scale are Pound's translations of Chinese poetry, which have very little to do with the usual notion of fidelity to the original, but which have become important for modern English literature because of their innovative character. Byron's popularity in the East confirms this translation paradigm. His *Giaour*, translated by Adam Mickiewicz in 1834, has become a 'Polish' poem, and as such has been taught to generations of Polish students.

The question raised by these unusually successful translations is: under what circumstances does a foreign text becomes an important part of the receiving culture? Is it determined by the text itself, or by the genius of the translator? Do social factors, the indefinable 'Zeitgeist', play an important part in the creation and dissemination of a translated text; or are we dealing here with pure chance? Research undertaken in the field of Translation Studies has shown that the phenomenon of

---

[5]   This phenomenon has been extensively discussed in the field of Translation Studies. See, for instance, *Translation, History, Culture*, ed. S. Bassnett and A. Lefevere (London, 1995).

translation is a complex one, and that there is no simple paradigm or method to foretell which text and whose translation may become an important contribution to the receiving culture.

The Slav reception of English Romanticism is good example of how complicated the process of literary and cultural transfer may be. There are essentially three English authors of that period who have attracted real attention in the East. These are: James Macpherson with his Celtic forgeries, Walter Scott, and Lord Byron. From an English perspective this is a bizarre canon, but from the European perspective it is quite logical. In all three cases European literary fame preceded translation. Because English was not widely spoken in the Slavic lands at the beginning of the nineteenth century, the English Romantics were first available to East European readers either in French or in German. The first Czech translations of these poets were via German intermediaries, while the Poles and Russians translated from the French.

The notion of what was and what was not a translation in the early nineteenth century was quite different from ours, which makes it difficult to define how important these translations were for the later assimilation of the authors into Slav cultures. Translation at that time was more closely related to what we would call today 'imitation'. Although scholars nowadays like to be precise about how one form of rewriting differs from another, few translators and writers of the last century felt compelled to define the boundaries between the two. It was not unsual to find fragments of Byron's poems incorporated into some-body else's work without acknowledgment, or to read poems footnoted 'after Byron', 'after reading Byron' and 'imitated from Byron'. Walter Scott's novels went through even more complicated transformations, depending on which 'pirated' French or German version served as the source text for the East European translation. Polish, Czech and Russian scholars have produced detailed bibliographical lists of all Byron trans-lations,[6] only to acknowledge that almost none of these early efforts have survived as literary texts. The translations which have survived are those in which Byron was domesticated, and was able to enter the blood-stream of national literatures. The case of Mickiewicz's *Giaour* is a prime example, but similar cases occurred in Bohemia (Macha's

---

6   See, P. Kuhiwczak, 'Byron w Polsce' (1816–1939), unpublished doctoral dissertation presented at the University of Warsaw, 1985. B. Manek, *Prvni ceske preklady Byronovy poezie* (Prague, 1991). V.M. Zhirmunskii, *Bairon i Pushkin* (Leningrad, 1924).

translations) and in Russia (with translations and adaptations by Lermontov and Pushkin).

Lermontov, again, is a useful case to look at if we want to understand how this textual 'domestication' comes about. Lermontov wrote two poems closely related to Byron's *Hebrew Melodies*. The first was written in 1830 and appeared in 1844 under the title *A Hebrew Melody* (although Lermontov originally intended to call it 'The Star, after Byron's *The Sun of the Sleepless*') The second poem Lermontov wrote in 1836, under the same title, *A Hebrew Melody*, and with the note, 'after Byron'. The question which would primarily occupy most modern critics would be: are the two poems translations or are they original? In two major editions of Lermontov's poetry published in Russia[7] both poems are classified as lyrics, since the editors do not differentiate between original writing and translations. In a major bilingual Russian-English volume of Lermontov's verse, Anatolii Liberman respects the Russian classification and lists the first *Hebrew Melody* under 'Lyrics'.[8] (The 1836 *Hebrew Melody* is not included in this collection.) So far, so good, but one cannot say much about translation without looking at the textual details. In the editorial comment appended to Liberman's translation of the 1830 *Hebrew Melody* (*Ia vidal inogda . . .*) we read that none of of Byron's lyrics is related rhythmically to Lermontov's poem, but *Sun of the Sleepless* is thematically close to it. Certainly both poets use the setting of a night sky to express their thoughts:

Byron:

> *Sun of the Sleepless*
> Sun of the sleepless! Melancholy star!
> Whose tearful beam glows tremulously far,
> That show'st the darkness thou canst not dispel,
> How like art thou to joy remember'd well!
> So gleams the past, the light of other days,
> Which shines, but warms not with its powerless rays;
> A night-beam Sorrow watcheth to behold,
> Distinct, but distant – clear, but oh, how cold![9]

[7] See, *Polnoe Sobranie Sochinenii Iu..M. Lermontova*, ed. D.I. Abramovich (Sankt Peterburg, 1913), and M. Lermontov, *Polnoe Sobrane Stikhotvoreni*, ed. Ia..A. Andreev (Leningrad, 1989).

[8] M. Lermontov, *Major Poetical Works*.

[9] Byron, *The Complete Poetical Works*, lines 1–8.

Lermontov:

A Hebrew Melody

I have seen from afar how a glittering star
  Has slept in a motionless bay;
But a breeze or a gust – and the silvery dust
  In a moment is carried away.

The reflection will sink, and you err if you think
  That close are the flash and the stream;
Your shadow will spread, and the light will be dead –
  Move away if you look for the gleam.

So it happens to most that, enticed by a ghost,
  We chase our enjoyment in vain;
We discover its shape . . . and the ghost will escape!
  But deceived we shall see it again.[10]

Even taking into account the shortcomings of Liberman's translation (in rhythm and tone), we can clearly see that Lermontov's way of using the setting differs from Byron's. It is true that both poems contain thoughts evoked by an optical illusion, but while Byron is interested in the distance starlight covers before reaching earth, Lermontov's thoughts turn on the fugitive nature of starlight reflected from the surface of water. Lermontov acknowledges the connection with Byron by giving the poem one of Byron's titles, not from fear of seeming to plagiarise, but to show that he is borrowing from Byron those features of his lyrical poetry which are not available in the Russian tradition. In this sense, Byron is playing the same role in Lermontov's artistic development that Catullus plays in Byron's.[11]

The 1836 Hebrew Melody (Dusha moia mrachna) is a much more conventional case of what is commonly understood as translation. At the basic, syntactic level, this poem corresponds closely to Byron's My Soul is Dark. The opening sentence of Lermontov's poem is a direct translation of the first sentence of Byron's lyric. Although the poem is not to be found in Liberman's edition, in an editorial comment appended to the first Hebrew Melody Liberman notes that Lermontov's translation of My Soul is Dark 'is not accurate, but it is one of his best

---

[10] M. Lermontov, Major Poetical Works, lines 1–12.
[11] See Byron's translations and imitations from Catullus in The Hours of Idleness (1806).

lyrics'.[12] When we compare this with his remark on the first *Hebrew Melody* (that the poem owes much to Byron), we see how confusing translation is for modern critics, and how much clearer the situation was only 150 years ago.

In their search for a methodology to provide an easy and clear-cut definition of where translation ends and imitation begins, many modern critics have abandoned common sense and their belief in the validity of good judgement. For the early nineteenth-century critic there would be nothing strange about the fact that a translation can become a good poem in its own right, but for some modern critics, a poem which is related to a foreign original cannot be seen as an achievement in itself. While commenting on Lermontov's 'inaccuracy' in translating from Byron, Liberman does not refer back to the original text; but it is only detailed textual analysis that can enable us to decide whether the inaccuracy is intentional, an artistic device, or simply ordinary carelessness. Lermontov's text is certainly not a word-for-word translation. The first four lines of his and Byron's lyrics read as follows:

Byron:

> My soul is dark – oh! quickly string
>   The harp I yet can brook to hear;
> And let thy gentle fingers fling
>   Its melting murmurs o'er mine ear.[13]

Lermontov:

> Dusha moia mrachna. Skorei pevets, skorei!
> (My soul is dark. Make haste, my bard, make haste!)
> Vot arfa zolotaia:
> (There is the harp of gold:)
> Puskai persti tvoi, promchavshisia po nei
> (Let your fingers, running over it,)
> Probudiat v strunakh zvuki raia
> (Awaken sounds of paradise in the strings.)[14]

The differences are obvious: for instance, in Lermontov's poem the harp is 'gold', and Byron's 'melting murmurs' have become 'sounds

---

[12] M. Lermontov, *Major Poetical Works*, p. 470.
[13] Byron, *The Complete Poetical Works*, lines 1–4.
[14] *Polnoye Sobranye Sotchineniy Y.M. Lermontova*, lines 1–4 (literal translation is mine – PK)

of paradise'. Some differences in the poem as a whole result from Lermontov's free choice, while elsewhere, the constraints of the Russian language and literary convention have forced the translator to depart from word-for-word precision. To call a translation which is clearly built on the 'sense for sense' principle 'inaccurate' is not particularly helpful, especially if these inaccuracies have contributed to the literary quality of one of Lermontov's best lyrics. But if this *Hebrew Melody* is classified as a not-so-good translation and a very good lyric, what can be said about the first *Hebrew Melody*? Is it a translation, imitation, or just one of Lermontov's less successful original poems?

What this kind of analysis tells us is that whenever a foreign writer's works, or a new literary form, are being assimilated into another national tradition, we do well to avoid categorising the process in terms of strict definitions. The process is a long one, with many transitional stages. What gets borrowed and assimilated is in most cases unpredictable: it depends very much on what the importing culture has in short supply and needs to find somewhere else. Byron's role in Eastern Europe is an interesting one, because he seems to have satisfied many diverse needs there in the first decades of the nineteenth century. As a critic has usefully observed, 'Although the enthusiasm for Byron's personality caught on all over Europe, the appeal of the poet whom Goethe hailed as the herald of world literature varied from nation to nation, in that each picked out that part of Byron's *oeuvre* most congenial to himself.'[15] It is true that many young East European poets learned their skills by translating and imitating Byron's lyrics in the same way Lermontov did. But otherwise East European tastes were varied, and sometimes they clashed. Adam Mickiewicz was very much taken with the characters from Byron's romantic tales, and he used them as models for his Polish and Lithuanian patriots, with their vague pasts, and highly obscure personal motivation (in the romantic tales *Grazyna* and *Konrad Wallenrod*). But what Mickiewicz so appreciated in the English poet, Alexander Pushkin later deplored. He compares Byron's characters to Shakespeare's dismissively in a letter to a friend:

How paltry is Byron as tragedian in comparison with him! This Byron who never conceived but one sole character (women do not have any character; they have passions in their youth; and this is why it is so easy to paint them), this Byron, then, has parceled out among his characters such-and-such a trait of his own character; his pride

15 H.G. Schenk, *The Mind of European Romantics* (London, 1966), p. 147.

to one, his hate to another, his melancholy to a third, etc., and thus out of one complete, gloomy, and energetic character he has made several insignificant characters – there is no tragedy in that.[16]

Pushkin's own characters – particularly Eugene Onegin – clearly show his contempt for Byronic heroes. But while he rejected Byron's characters, Pushkin appreciated and often adapted the narrative form of Byron's long poems, and he mentions *Don Juan* several times in connection with his own work. *Eugene Onegin* is often referred to by critics as a 'novel in verse';[17] though if we compare it to Byron's work we see that, apart from its rounder characters, Pushkin's poem is also distinguished by a more disciplined structure. The ramblings of *Childe Harold's Pilgrimage* and *Don Juan* are not here, and the internal logic of a well-structured story line is definitely Pushkin's contribution. The stanza of Pushkin's poem is also different from Byron's. Pushkin rejected Byron's *ottava rima*, and modelled his stanza on the Italian sonnet with a single definite rhyme scheme (ABABCCDDEFFEGG) combining feminine and masculine rhymes. In this way he could exploit the flexibility of the sonnet stanza (in some parts of the work he was closer to the 6 plus 8 division, in others he was closer to the English sonnet).[18] He could also vary end-stopped lines with enjambement, allowing him rigid and flexible sentence structure at the same time.

In its elegance, lightness and touch of irony, *Eugene Onegin* is often considered much closer to classicism than to Romanticism, and one may wonder whether it is appropriate to link Pushkin's work with Byron's at all. But Byron's Romanticism is not unproblematic either. On many occasions the poet expressed his deep admiration for Pope, and some of his better achievements – *Beppo* is a good example – are more rooted in classical tradition than in the Romantic reaction to it. In his essay on Byron's satire, F.R. Leavis locates Byron more properly at the end of the eighteenth-century tradition than at the beginning of Romanticism;[19] and since Pushkin was also the poet who most successfully bridged the two literary epochs in Russia, readers had no difficulty

---

16 *The Letters of Alexander Pushkin*, trans. J.T. Shaw (Bloomington, 1963), vol. 1, p. 277.
17 See, for instance, J. Bayley, *Pushkin. A Comparative Commentary* (Cambridge, 1971).
18 For an extensive analysis of Pushkin's versification, see A.D.P. Briggs, *A. Pushkin. A Critical Study* (London, 1983).
19 F.R. Leavis, 'Byron's Satire', in *Byron. A Collection of Critical Essays*, ed. P. West (New York, 1963), pp. 83–88.

in accepting Byron as both classic and Romantic. The usefulness of Byron as a literary model for Slavs derived from precisely the idiosyncratic and transitional nature of his poetic style.

But if Byron's *oeuvre* was so carefully scrutinized and 'pillaged' by Slav poets, was there anything in it that met with a less than enthusiastic reception? One element of his poetry which was consistently played down in the East was his orientalism. In fact, the whole phenomenon of Orientalism, which played such a big part in English Romanticism, found very few followers among Slav poets. Byron's 'Eastern' tales were read, translated and imitated much more for their Byronic characters than for their exotic flavour – though many preferred Byron's images of the East to what other English writers had to offer. Neither Beckford's eccentric *Vathek* nor Coleridge's *Kubla Khan* attracted much attention. The reason for this indifference was simple: for the Slavs, unlike the English, the Orient was not a figment of the imagination but a reality. Jan Potocki, whose *Saragossa Manuscripts* have only just been 'discovered' by western readers, was publishing his literary accounts of travels to Mongolia, Turkey, Egypt and the Caucasus throughout the 1780s and 1790s. The centuries-long history of Polish and Russian contacts with the Ottoman Empire made it impossible for writers to fantasize about the East as freely as Beckford could fantasize in England. Both Mickiewicz and Pushkin had first-hand experience of the East: Pushkin was exiled to the Caucasus, and Mickiewicz, after years of Russian and French exile, died in Turkey, while attempting to organize Polish legions to aid the Turks against the Russians.

Both Pushkin and Mickiewicz wrote collections of beautiful and subtle lyrics relating to the places they visited in the East, but they had few illusions about the orient. In a letter to another Russian poet, Piotr Viazemskii, Pushkin emphasizes the difference between a genuine interest in the Orient and a shallow imitation:

> The Eastern style was a model for me, insofar as it is possible for us, rational, cold Europeans. Apropos again, do you know why I dislike Moore? Because he is excessively Eastern. He imitates childlishly and in an ugly manner the childishness and ugliness of Saadi, Hafiz, and Mohammed. A European, even in the rapture of Oriental splendour, must preserve the taste and eye of a European. That is why Byron is so charming in *The Giaour*, in *The Bride of Abydos*, etc.[20]

---

[20] *The Letters of Alexander Pushkin*, vol. 1, p. 214.

The question we have been trying to answer is: why was it Byron, and not the other English Romantics, who was so keenly 'appropriated' by Slav poets? Historical circumstances and Byron's colourful biography can only explain the 'lower', more sensational and purely imitative element of Byronism – what we might call Byronic fever. The reasons for the 'higher' type of Byronism must be attributed to the multifaceted nature of Byron's poetic style. It may still seem paradoxical, though, that Wordsworth and Coleridge, who wrote before Byron, and are now considered central figures of English Romanticism, should not have appealed to the Slavs – but on closer consideration, one can understand that neither their vaunted return to 'the common language of men', nor their liberation of the imagination, were ideas which the Slav literary milieu particularly needed. For historical and social reasons the Slav nations were much closer to their rural roots than the English, and folk culture found its public role in rebuilding Czech cultural identity, for instance, or laying the foundations for nineteenth-century theories about the common cultural identity of all Slavic people. At a more pragmatic level, one also cannot overlook the fact that the eastern borderlands of Poland, with their astonishing mixture of cultures, traditions and languages, provided a much more fertile ground for the romantic imagination than the Lake District. Poets like Adam Mickiewicz turned this rich cultural heritage into literary form; and to his own suprise, Mickiewicz's first volume of poetry *Ballads and Romances* (1823) – which can be seen as the Polish equivalent of *Lyrical Ballads* – found many buyers among simple people. As the author remarked: 'Kitchen maids and ladies' maids were the first to buy.'[21] The evidence available in England tells us that the simple people of the Lake District did not have the same positive attitude towards the English bard.[22] But the dispute here is not about the closeness of these two poets to the people, but about how raw material gets turned into a literary work. Although Mickiewicz's 'common people' are as stylized as Wordsworth's, he does not attempt to draw the reader's attention to the fact that these people are 'simple' or 'unfortunate'. The reader is under the illusion that the voices of simple maids and village boys are directly audible, without the intervention of the narrator. Thus, in the famous ballad *Romanticism*, the mad and unfortunate servant girl is not patron- ized by the narrator, but is juxtaposed with a rational professor who does

[21] K. Pruszynski, *Adam Mickiewicz* (London, 1950), p. 21.
[22] See, for instance, H.D. Rawnsley, *Reminiscences of Wordsworth among the Peasantry of Westmoreland* (London, 1968).

not understand her state of mind. The girl may be simple and insane, but her insanity is the result of a personal tragedy that we – rational readers, and the 'simple' people present in the ballad – should be capable of understanding:

> Thus with endearing words, caresses vain,
> The maiden stumbles; pleads and cries aloud:
> Seeing her fall, hearing her voice of pain,
> Gathers the curious crowd.
> Gathers the crowd and murmers: 'Say a prayer!
> Here is Karusia, Jasio's promised bride;
> His ghost must be here, walking at her side,
> He loved her so,' the simple folk declare.
>
> And I – I cannot question what they say;
> I hear, and I believe. I weep and pray.
> 'Hark, maiden! Hark! an old man calls aloud;
> 'Listen to me!' he shouts to all the crowd;
> 'My eyes are true, my spectacles are clear,
> And I see nothing here.'
>
> 'Ghosts are a figment of the vulgar throng,
> By folly shaped upon the forge of dreams;
> The maiden gibbers nonsense – idle, wrong;
> The stupid rabble utterly blasphemes.'
>
> I answer modestly: 'The maid can feel,
> The common people to their faith are true:
> Feeling and faith to me far more reveal
> Than eyes and spectacles, though learned, do.[23]

Mickiewicz's technique can be compared to that of Chopin: nobody doubts there are folk motifs in his music, but it is also obvious that they are highly stylized. Under such circumstances the artist is not expected to put forward either his personal view of the people's simplicity or to supply examples of social realism in his work.

In this respect, Wordsworth's poetry is far removed from the Slav tradition. He, like Mickiewicz and Pushkin, finds madness a good

---

[23] *Konrad Wallenrod and Other Writings of Adam Mickiewicz*, trans. J. Parish, D. Prall Radin, G.R. Noyes (Berkeley, 1925), lines 44–65. This translation does not do full justice to the original poem, and neither do the other two translations produced since 1925. Therefore the reader will have to trust my word concerning the artistic quality of the Polish original.

subject for poetry, but for very different reasons. There are two poems in the *Lyrical Ballads* which are devoted to ordinary people's unusual states of mind, but here the obtrusive narratorial interventions make for a quite different treatment: Wordsworth himself permeates the works. Although the stated aim of the *Lyrical Ballads* was to vindicate the people and their language, the intention is one thing and what one reads in the poems another. Wordsworth usually provides a much more realistic characterization of the country people than Mickiewicz, but the kind of details we are given raise pity rather than respect. The mad mother from the ballad of the same title is both mentally unbalanced and physically unattractive:

> Her eyes are wild, her head is bare,
> The sun has burnt her coal-black hair,
> Her eyebrows have a rusty stain,
> And she came far from over the main.[24]

But if her irrational (and perhaps too coherent) narrative is a credible result of 'madness', the irrationality of the characters in another 'mad' poem – *The Idiot Boy* – seems only to be another aspect of the fact that the author conceives them as simple folk. How else can one explain Betty's decision to send her son for the doctor, only to follow him when it becomes clear that he is not able to accomplish his mission? Betty's friend Susan, who apparently cannot be left alone, is abandoned in turn by the boy and Betty. And despite the opening drama of the situation, which leads the mother to burden her insane child with an impossible task, there are no consequences for the plot. Susan recovers as a result of intense mental activity:

> Long Susan lay deep lost in thought,
> And many dreadful fears beset her,
> Both for her messenger and nurse;
> And as her mind grew worse and worse,
> Her body it grew better.[25]

The logical weakness of the poem may be partly due to the fact that Wordsworth's attitude to 'Romantic' notions of madness is clearly

---

[24] Wordsworth and Coleridge, *Lyrical Ballads 1798*, ed. W.J.B Owens (Oxford, 1969), lines 1–4.
[25] Wordsworth and Coleridge, *Lyrical Ballads 1798*, lines 422–27.

ironic, and John's inarticulateness and passivity are stressed in contra-distinction to the illusions other Romantics preferred to harbour:

> Unto his horse, that's feeding free,
> He seems, I think, the rein to give;
> Of moon or stars he takes no heed;
> Of such we in romances read,
> – 'Tis Johnny! Johnny! as I live.[26]

But while acknowledging the irony, we cannot disregard the impression that Wordsworth's view of simple people is that of someone seeing them from a vast distance. On the evidence of this, his theoretical assumptions about the value of folk culture are simply theories, and what emerges between the lines is a quiet contempt for real rural life. Perhaps this is another reason why Wordsworth's poetry has not travelled well to the East. Certainly Wordsworth has never been appropriated or domesticated in Slav countries in the same way as Byron: it is up to the western reader to decide whether this insensibility is the Slavs' own problem – or whether Wordsworth's greatness does look more problem-atic when viewed outside its usual context.

It is often claimed that poetry never travels well in foreign trans-lation. But the reality is more complex, as we have seen. And when we examine cases of both successful and unsuccessful translation, we have an invaluable tool for shaping a more objective perspective on national literary canons, which are often formed by local and deeply subjective cultural, political and literary forces.

---

26 Wordsworth and Coleridge, *Lyrical Ballads 1798*, lines 362–67.

Writtin in the Langage of Scottis Natioun: Literary Translation into Scots

JOHN CORBETT

Introduction

THERE HAVE BEEN TWO KEY PERIODS in the history of literary translation into Scots: the sixteenth and twentieth centuries. The sixteenth century marked the full flowering of a distinct Scottish literary tradition. Although looking south to England and overseas to continental Europe for models and inspiration, Scottish poets and dramatists developed a peculiarly Scottish treatment of their subject matter, and they did so in a fully-functional lowland Scots vernacular, as acceptable to their courtly patrons in Edinburgh as to the burghers in the towns and the peasants in the fields. The sixteenth century would be the last century in which this situation would be so. The loss of the court to England in the early seventeenth century and the absorption of the Scottish nation into the British state had linguistic as well as political consequences, not least the eventual rise in Scotland of a prestigious standard language which looked south for its norms of linguistic politeness and then correctness. However, in a second renaissance in the twentieth century, many Scottish poets and dramatists have again turned to translation into Scots, with perhaps even more energy and enthusiasm than before. This paper considers some of the correspondences and distinctions between these two great periods of literary translation into Scots.

The Sixteenth Century

The father of Scottish translation is Gavin Douglas (1475–1522), and any consideration of later translations into Scots must recognise the influence of his stated beliefs and his practice. He completed his translation of Virgil's *Aeneid* in 1513, at the request of his patron and kinsman, Henry, Lord Sinclair. Sinclair's insistence that Douglas translate 'Virgill or Homeir' was only one factor in the poet's decision to render the *Aeneid* into Scots; another was the perceived damage to the source text perpetrated by William Caxton's translation into English of a French version of the tale. In the Prologue to the First Book, Douglas gives a vivid description of his reaction to Caxton's rendition:

> I red his wark with harmys at my hart
> That syk a buke but sentens or engyne
> Suld be intitillit eftir the poet devyne;
> His ornate golden versis mair than gilt
> I spittit for dispyte to se swa spilt
> With sych a wyght, quhilk trewly be myne entent
> Knew never thre wordis at all quhat Virgill ment –
> Sa fer he chowpis I am constrenyt to flyte.[1]
>
> (Book 1, lines 146–53)

The general thrust of Douglas's attack is clear: the Scottish poet wishes to clear Virgil from guilt by association with the poetic inadequacies of Caxton's feeble prose, which lacks 'substance and ingenuity'. The Prologue goes on to detail further objections to Caxton's translation: he omits whole books, changes plot details, and dwells on the love affair of Dido and Aeneas in 'prolixt and tedyus fasson'. Not only is the verse tarnished, the whole structure of the source text is altered, in such a way that it seems to Douglas to result in a travesty of a revered text. However, Caxton is perhaps unfortunate to be singled out for Douglas's attack. As Bawcutt has noted, 'Through Caxton's *Eneydos* Douglas is criticizing popular medieval treatments of the *Aeneid* and popular notions of translation.'[2] Douglas, in the opening of his translation, is concerned more generally with raising the intellectual stakes of translation, and he demands, wherever possible, fidelity to the source text in the practice of it:

> Traiste weill to follow a fixt sentens or mater
> Is mair practike, deficill and far strater,
> Thocht thyne engyne beyn elevate and hie,
> Than forto write all ways at liberte.
>
> (Book 1, lines 289–92)

Various critics have discussed the extent to which Douglas manages to

---

1 All references to Douglas's *Eneados* are from *Selections from Gavin Douglas*, ed. David Coldwell (Clarendon Press, Oxford, 1964)
2 P. Bawcutt, *Gavin Douglas, A Critical Study* (Edinburgh University Press, Edinburgh, 1976), p. 81.

hold to his precepts.[3] However, Douglas anticipates these criticisms, recognising that complete fidelity is impossible, but that the translator should work within the constraints imposed by historical or linguistic obscurity, or the demands of the target language:

> And thus I am constrenyt als neir I may
> To hald hys vers and go nane other way,
> Les sum history, subtell word or the ryme
> Causith me mak digressioun sum tyme.
>
> (Book 1, lines 303–06)

At the start of the Scottish tradition in literary translation, then, we find a concern for fidelity to a classical text, and for the adequate representation of the gifts of its author. We also find an awareness of the distinctiveness of the target vernacular, in particular its distinctiveness from the language of Caxton and his countryfolk. A brief illustration of the Scottish poet's style, in comparison with a later English translator, Dryden, is given by Coldwell.[4] The Latin text is as follows:

> navem in conspectu nullam, tris litore cervos
> prospicit errantis; hos tota armenta sequuntur
> a tergo et longum per vallis pascitur agmen.   (I. 184–86)

Douglas renders these lines as tetrameter couplets:

> Na schip he saw, bot sone he gat a syght
> Of thre hartis waverand by the cost syde,
> Quham at the bak, throu out the gravis wide,
> The mekil herdis followit in a rowt
> And pasturit all the large valle about.
>
> (Book 1, iv. lines 48–52)

---

[3] Bawcutt (op. cit.), pp. 124–27 summarises some of the criticisms, coming to the conclusion that in terms of contemporary scholarship, Douglas's translation 'does not distort the proportions of the *Aeneid* nor fundamentally alter Virgil's thought' (p. 127). Her close analysis of Douglas's use of his sources, particularly Ascensius's commentary of c.1500 (pp. 96–102), supports her view.

[4] Coldwell, ed. (op. cit.), introduction, pp. x–xi. Coldwell glosses the Latin as 'He observed no ship in sight, but three stags wandering on the shore; whole herds followed behind them and in a long line graze through the valley.'

The tone of this translation, to modern eyes, is straightforward and unaffected, lacking the grandiose quality of Dryden's high-style rendition:

> No Vessels were in view: But, on the Plain
> Three beamy Stags command a Lordly Train
> Of branching Heads; the more ignoble Throng
> Attend their stately Steps, and slowly graze along.
>
> (I. 259–62)

Where Dryden anthropomorphises the deer into lords and vassals, Douglas holds closer to the register of the source text, offering a plainer version. As we shall see, in later translations into Scots, it is this lack of pretentiousness which translators often value – as a medium of translation, Scots offers a target language which is largely free of much of the cultural baggage of the post-Union English literary tradition. But, as we shall also see, it has a baggage of its own.

Douglas's translation of the *Aeneid* is one of the earliest texts in which a sharp distinction is made between 'Inglis' and 'Scottis'.[5] Scottish poets of the fourteenth and fifteenth centuries routinely referred to the vernacular tongue as 'Inglis'; for example, Douglas's contemporary, William Dunbar, praises Chaucer's facility in 'oure tong . . . oure Inglisch' ('The Goldyn Targe', lines 254, 259). Elsewere, in 'The Flyting of Dunbar and Kennedie', Dunbar praises his own vernacular 'Inglis', while deriding the Gaelic, or 'Ersche' of his west-coast compatriot, Walter Kennedy. In general, in Scotland, the terms 'Inglis' and 'Scottis' continued to be used interchangeably throughout the sixteenth century and beyond. Douglas, however, has none of this. His reverence for Chaucer is less keen than Dunbar's (he notes that 'My mastir Chauser gretly Virgill offendit'; Bk 1, line 410). Moreover, Douglas's decription of 'the langage of Scottis natioun' (Bk 1, line 103) dwells on the differences between it and the southern variety – to the extent that he treats 'Inglis' as if it were on a par with French, all vernaculars, of course, paling into insignificance beside Latin, the 'maste perfite langage fyne' (Bk 1, line 381). Douglas recognises that the linguistic resources peculiar to lowland Scots would be inadequate to the task of rendering

---

5 J.D. McClure, 'Scottis, Inglis, Suddroun: Language Labels and Language Attitudes' in *Proceedings of the Third International Conference on Scottish Language and Literature (Medieval and Renaissance)*, ed. Roderick J. Lyall and Felicity Riddy (Stirling/Glasgow, 1981), pp. 52–69.

Virgil's text; but he was also working within a literary tradition which valued 'aureation', that is, a poetic style which placed value on aesthetically-pleasing vocabulary, usually borrowed from Latin, sometimes via French. The literary language of Scotland was to some extent a 'synthetic' language, incorporating elements from foreign sources both for concepts alien to renaissance Scotland, and also for pure decoration.[6] Unlike his contemporaries and predecessors, Douglas sees fit to apologise for this poetic strategy:

> Lyk as in Latyn beyn Grew termys sum,
> So me behufyt quhilum or than be dum
> Sum bastard Latyn, French or Inglys oys
> Quhar scant was Scottis – I had nane other choys.
>
> (Book 1, lines 115–18)

The recognition here is that the language of the translated *Aeneid* is going to be, unavoidably, a mixture, a hybrid. The presence of Greek terms in Latin offers a precedent for this, but it is more significant that Douglas finds it necessary at all to draw attention to the fundamental Scottishness of his medium of translation. It is difficult to avoid the conclusion that the project of translating Virgil from Latin into Scots was seen by Douglas as a nationalist one, despite the fact that there is little in Douglas's personal background to indicate any hostility to England. Indeed, as McClure has observed, 'his influence on Scottish politics was consistently pro-English, and he eventually owed his Bishopric of Dunkeld to the machinations of Margaret Tudor and her brother Henry VIII'.[7] McClure suggests that Douglas's awareness of the distinctiveness of Scots resulted from a period of residence in England, where, he supposes, Douglas might have been struck by the comparatively greater divergence of spoken English and Scots. However, it is not necessary to suppose that Scottish patriotism must necessarily be equivalent to anglophobia – Douglas's English sympathies and connections need not prevent his work having the goal of furthering the cause of his own nation and its distinctive vernacular. In his poem, 'The Palice of Honour', Douglas maintains his insistence on the separateness of the poets of England and Scotland,[8] and this emphasis on distinctive

---

6   See, for example, Bengt Ellenberger, *The Latin Element in the Vocabulary of the Earlier Makars Henryson and Dunbar* (CWK Gleerup, Lund, 1977).

7   McClure (op. cit.), p. 61

8   Bawcutt (op. cit.), p. 42

Scottish and English identities is a consistent feature of his work. It is this emphasis which marks Douglas out as the predecessor of all the translators into Scots who follow him: he was an intellectual, both learned and rigorous; he wrote in the Scottish vernacular at a time when it was the fully functional language of the Scottish nation, used for all purposes, domestic and public; and he stressed the separate and distinctive identity of the Scottish people and their tongue.

As the sixteenth century progressed, the political goals of translation were to come to the fore, while the desire for rigorous fidelity was to decline. Literature and politics at the end of the sixteenth century merged in the person of the young king, James VI. While governing Scotland, he gathered around himself a group of poets known as the 'Castalian Band', and at the age of seventeen James published a guide to poets, *Essayes of a Prentise in the Devine Arte of Poesie*, incorporating the *Reulis and cautelis* ['Rules and Cautions'] *to be observit and eschewit in Scottis Poesie*.[9] The nationalist project of late sixteenth-century literary activity is explicit in James's treatise, and he, like Douglas, draws attention to the differences between the Scots and English languages. Indeed, his motivation for writing his guide is partly to provide Scots poets with the kind of advice which had been available to writers in other languages, including English:

> The uther cause is, that as for thame that hes written in it [i.e. about the rules of poetry] of late, there hes never ane of thame written in our language. For albeit sindrie hes written of it in English, quhilk is lykest to our language, yit we differ from thame in sindrie reulis of poesie, as ye will find be experience.

In other ways, however, James seems, at least at first sight, to be inimical to Douglas. This is particularly true of James's apparent championing of originality, and his warning to poets to avoid translation:

> Bot sen Invention is ane of the cheif vertewis in a poete, it is best that ye invent your awin subject, your self, and not to compose of sene subjectis. Especially, translating any thing out of uther language, quhilk doing, ye not onely essay not your awin ingyne of Inventioun,

9 Quotations from the *Reulis and Cautelis* are taken from the selection in R.D.S. Jack's anthology *Scottish Prose 1550–1700* (Calder and Boyars, London 1971), pp. 108–11.

bot be the same meanes, ye are bound, as to a staik, to follow that
buikis phrasis, quhilk ye translate.

However, as Jack has argued, James's cautions should not, perhaps, be
seen as the warnings of a cultural separatist against translation in
general, but rather they should be seen as recognising the responsibilities and difficulties inherent in the translation process, in particular the
disciplined subjugation of one's own 'ingyne of Inventioun' in the
service of the source text, whose 'phrasis' must be respected.[10] This
reading is supported by James's own practice, and by the encouragement
he gave to fellow poets. The *Reulis and Cautelis* itself is much influenced
by foreign models, particularly Du Bellay and Gascoigne. Du Bellay was,
in fact, one of a number of foreign poets invited by James to visit
Edinburgh, and the Scottish king translated and published a version of
Du Bartas' *Uranie*. In the role of Maecenas to his Castalian Band of
poets, James actively encouraged William Fowler to translate Petrarch's
Trionfi and Machiavelli's *Il Principe*; and also John Stewart of Baldynneis
to produce a version of Ariosto's *Orlando Furioso*. Stewart's fine version,
Roland Furious, makes an illuminating comparison with Douglas's
Eneados, partly because it can be attacked in very similar terms to those
in which Douglas attacked Caxton. Stewart used a French source,
Desportes' *Roland Furieux*, as his primary intermediary text, and excuses
his 'abbregement' on the grounds that it should be seen as an adaptation
rather than a translation:

> This work of myn behuifs me scher it so;
> Quhyls heir, quhyls thair, quhyls fordwart and behind,
> The historie all interlest I find
> With syndrie sayings of so great delyt,
> That singlie most I from the rest out spind.   (Canto V)[11]

Like Caxton, then, Stewart alters the shape of the source text: it is
wider-ranging than Desportes' version, but not so extensive as Ariosto's
poem. However, Stewart cannot be faulted on his 'Inglys gros'; his Scots
verse displays a mannered virtuosity that combines energy and
ornamentation, qualities that can be seen in this brief quotation from

[10] See R.D.S. Jack, *The Italian Influence on Scottish Literature* (Edinburgh
University Press, Edinburgh, 1972), pp. 55–56.
[11] See R.D.S. Jack (ibid.), p. 58.

Canto 11,[12] in which Medor expresses his love for the beautiful Angelique:

> O herbis greine and prettie plants formois
> O limpid wattir springing suave and cleir
> O cave obscuir aggriabill to thois
> Quho wold tham cuil in thy fresche umber deir,
> Quhair Angelique maist beutifull but peir
> In vayne desyrd be uthers monie mo,
> Oft nakit lay betwix my armes heir.
>
> (Canto 11, lines 233–39)

Stewart's own poetic preferences are here illustrated: the rhetorical patterning, the dense alliteration, and the obvious rhythms. James's *Reulis and Cautelis* gives Stewart licence to depart from strict adherence to one's sources, in the service of 'Invention', or aesthetic effect in Scots. Douglas's reverence for his source text is great; and while James and his followers recognise and respect such reverence, they accord comparatively greater value to the opportunites that source texts afford for invention in the target language. If James, or Stewart, had attacked Caxton, it would not have been on the grounds of his departures from Virgil's poetic structure, it would have been purely on the grounds of his poor prose.

This has been, of course, a selective view of literary translation in the sixteenth century – however, the poets discussed here set the tone and the range of possibilities for translation practice in Scotland in the renaissance and well beyond. If Douglas set the standard by which later translators would be measured, then James and the Castalians stretched the possibilities, by making freer adaptations respectable again, even while giving due respect to the more disciplined, self-effacing tradition of close translation. The bond that unites Douglas and the Castalian translators is a nationalist one: Scots translation in the sixteenth century was increasingly a conscious attempt to place a distinctive Scottish literature in the pantheon of European literature, alongside Italian, French and the similar, but separate, English tradition. This project naturally suffered a blow at the beginning of the seventeenth century when Maecenas deserted the Castalians to become King James I of the new United Kingdom. Several of James's poets followed him

---

[12] In R.D.S. Jack, ed., *A Choice of Scottish Verse 1560–1660* (Hodder and Stoughton, London, 1978), p. 105.

south, and they continued their careers there, but the translation of the king from Edinburgh to London had profound consequences for a distinctive Scottish literary tradition, and indeed the continuing prestige of the Scots variety of language. The Scottish poets were absorbed into the vibrant English literary scene, and English norms were swiftly adopted. The only poet to remain active in Scotland, William Drummond of Hawthornden, was also concerned to write in acceptable English, and even James, late in life, revised and anglicised his own literary output, with the help of his son, Charles.[13]

The Scottish literary tradition, however, did not die out – but, for a while, it changed direction. With the departure of the court to England, literary poetry in Scots was no longer published, but in the towns and farms of Scotland, oral literature continued to flourish. Consequently, when in the eighteenth and nineteenth centuries distinct Scottish national identity again sought literary expression, it was to the oral tradition, the songs and ballads, that Ramsay, Fergusson, Burns, Scott, Hogg and Galt principally turned. The native was privileged above the foreign, as in Burns's lines from 'Tam o' Shanter', in which the dancing witches favour traditional Scottish music:

> Nae cotillion brent-new frae *France*,
> But hornpipes, jigs strathspeys and reels,
> Put life and mettle in their heels.   (lines 116–18)

It is significant that the most influential 'translation' of this period is James Thomson's rendition of the poetry of the Gaelic bard, Ossian: the barbaric 'Ersche' disparaged by William Dunbar had become the romanticised tongue of the exotic Highlander. The phenomenal success of the Scottish literary tradition in refashioning itself from its native resources is possibly responsible for the relative paucity of translation activity in this period. It is not until the twentieth century that poets and dramatists turned again in force to Europe and beyond for models and inspiration, and, as we shall see, the translators of the sixteenth century offer instructive parallels and contrasts to their modern counterparts.

---

[13] R.D.S. Jack, *The Italian Influence on Scottish Literature*, p. 90.

The Twentieth Century

If the coverage of sixteenth-century translation in Scotland, given above, is ruthlessly selective, then the present treatment of twentieth-century translation into Scots must be even more so. A small sample of the range of translations of European poetry into Scots (and English) can be seen in an anthology compiled by Peter France and Duncan Glen.[14] A recent anthology of work selected from the Scots literary magazine, *Lallans*, also shows a substantial proportion of translated work, as well as an essay by poet William Neill on the subject of translation into Scots,[15] and at least one full-length book is planned on the use of Scots in translation in the present century.[16] The tremendous upsurge in literary translation into Scots in modern times was largely inspired by the success of Hugh MacDiarmid, and in particular, the translations embedded into the long, philosophical narrative poem 'A Drunk Man Looks at the Thistle'.[17] In trying to revive a Scottish literature with an international scope, written in a Scots which could function as a full national language, MacDiarmid looked back to the internationalism and confident expression of the sixteenth century. He recommended the literary model of Dunbar rather than Burns; however, in some ways the translator, Douglas, would have been a more appropriate exemplar. Much of 'A Drunk Man Looks at the Thistle' is an address to Dostoevsky, and into this modernist collage are woven several poems, 'from the Russian of Alexander Blok', and others. The best known is Blok's 'The Lady Unknown', which begins:

> At darknin' hings abune the howff
> A weet and wild and eisenin' air.
> Spring's spirit wi' its waesome sough
> Rules owre the drucken stramash there.   (lines 169–72)

---

[14] Peter France and Duncan Glen, eds, *European Poetry in Scotland: An Anthology of Translations* (Edinburgh University Press, Edinburgh, 1989). Roughly half of the poems compiled in the anthology are in Scots.

[15] Neil R. McCallum and David Purves, eds, *Mak it New* (The Mercat Press, Edinburgh, 1995).

[16] Findlay, Bill, *The Use of Scots in Translation* (Scottish Cultural Press, Aberdeen, forthcoming).

[17] Quotations from 'A Drunk Man Looks at the Thistle' are taken from the annotated edition by Kenneth Buthlay (Scottish Academic Press, Edinburgh, 1987). The sources of the various 'translations' are carefully presented there.

However, as MacDiarmid's protagonist confesses to Dostoevsky elsewhere in the poem, 'I ken nae Russian and you ken nae Scots' (line
2224), and it has been shown that, as Stewart used an intermediary text
to translate Ariosto, so MacDiarmid used a bridging text to render Blok.
In the latter case, the intermediary text was in English – it was B.
Deutsch and A. Yarmolinsky's version in *Modern Russian Poetry:*[18]

> Of evenings hangs above the restaurant
> A humid, wild and heavy air.
> The Springtide spirit, brooding, pestilent,
> Commands the drunken outcries there. (lines 1–4)

Obviously, MacDiarmid is interested in more than internationalism in
his choice of source text and target language. The Russian source is as
much determined by the communist Scot's political sympathies as by
aesthetic appreciation. Yet the source text is integrated into the poem,
at the expense of literal translation, particularly at the point where the
narrator in the translation makes reference to the wife in the larger
poem:

> And ilka evenin' derf and serious
> (Jean ettles nocht o' this, puir lass),
> In liquor, raw, yet still mysterious,
> A'e freend's aye mirrored in my glass. (lines 185–88)

The Deutsch and Yarmolinsky translation is:

> And every evening, dazed and serious,
> I watch the same procession pass;
> In liquor, raw and yet mysterious
> One friend is mirrored in my glass. (lines 17–20)

The MacDiarmid version, then, in some ways is close to the literal
English translation, but at other times, as in line 186, there are
significant departures in the service of integration of the translation
into the wider text. The tension between invention and fidelity to one's
source is again apparent, with invention winning through.

The MacDiarmid version of the poem, however, is greatly superior
to its English crib, and it is worth considering why this should be so.

---

[18] London, 1923. Reprinted in Buthlay (op. cit.), pp. 19, 21.

One reason, I would suggest, is the target variety used – the fact that translations into Scots inevitably carry connotations of authenticity, or unaffected plain speaking, which are not so readily triggered by renditions into English. As we saw above, Coldwell made a similar point when comparing Dryden and Douglas. The semiotic value of the use of Scots for translation is, by and large, that is does, to modern eyes and ears, betoken a popular language that has a distinguished literary history. The irony is that, from Douglas to MacDiarmid, the Scots language used in translation has always been, to some extent, synthetic – a language variety that appeals to the language of the people, but that is essentially a literary creation and recreation. MacDiarmid famously, or notoriously, extended his native dialect by trawling through Jamieson's dictionary of Scots for archaisms, and introducing elements of Scots furth of his own locality. At its most synthetic, this high literary language has been dubbed 'Lallans', or 'Lowlands'. MacDiarmid's example has inspired several generations of 'modern makars', but the Lallans movement has also triggered a counter-reaction, by writers who see in Lallans a threat to Scots' appeal as a language of the people. These writers opt to stay closer to the regional and social varieties into which Scots has fragmented over the past four centuries. In the remainder of this paper, we shall consider the various options open to the present-day translator into Scots.

Douglas Young was an enthusiastic Lallans poet and translator, and a polemicist on behalf of a revived Scots. He translated the Gaelic poetry of his contemporay, Sorley Maclean, and in his versions of Aristophanes' *The Burdies* and *The Puddocks* he harks back to the tradition of classical translation, initiated by Gavin Douglas. However, in the intervening centuries between Douglas's first Prologue and the modern Renaissance, the social function of Scots had narrowed, literary tastes had changed in favour of the spontaneous and 'natural', and English had become, for the Lallans writers, much more threatening. In an address to a meeting of the Dunedin Society, chaired by Hugh MacDiarmid, Young states:

> First, it seems to me ridiculous to restrict oneself to words heard. It is important to keep contact with the living racy spoken language of all sorts and conditions of Scots, but no literary creator in English, Russian, or French would restrict himself to words heard. Words read may be as good as words heard, and even a Methuselah would never hear all the words which are still used. I even adopt words read in a dictionary, or words I make up for myself from Scots and kindred

roots by old Scots priciples, such as my words 'Ice-flumes' for glaciers.

Secondly, I think that enough harm has been done by the practice of Gawn Douglas and Allan Ramsay of introducing English vocables into Lallans. We have already too many strangers within our gates and are risking the loss of our citadel. It is just like the controversy about admitting Poles, Englishry, and such like to Scots citizenship. Admit a few of many nationalities, but do not allow too large a quota to any one breed of immigrant. If Lallans fails, coin something from Latin or Greek if you like, as King's English does; if all else fails admit a Hottentotism rather than another Anglicism. This should be our intransigent policy for the next five hundred years or so.[19]

There is an interesting set of tensions here: first of all, between the principles of openness, practised by Douglas and, up to a point, by Young, and the unsavoury tone of exclusive nationalism, which would put a quota on cosmopolitan influence, and a ban on English. And secondly, there is a tension between the appeal to historical authenticity and the project of creating a new language from a synthesis of regional varieties, augmented by loanwords, neologisms and archaisms. These tensions, however, are well-suited to Young's translation of Aristophanes, a version which incorporates modern Scottish references into the Greek text, as in this exchange between Aiakos and Dionysus:

Aiakos   Wha's there?
Dionysus Teuch guy Herakles.
Aiakos   Ye scunnersome, ootrageous skellum, you,
               mischievous villain, bluidie blagyart, you,
               You rave awa oor collie Cerberus,
               gruppit his thrapple and ran aff wi him.
               I've watched for you, and nou ye're fairly cotcht.
               The black whin-hertit craig o Styx bydes for ye,
               and Acheron's bluid-dreepan preecipice
               staunds sentinel, and Kokytos' rinnan hunds;
               the hunner-heidit boa-constrictor snake
               sall ryve your guts; the Loch Ness monsteress
               sall tear the lichties oot ye; your twa kidneys,
               wi aa your vital harigals, reeman wi bluid,

---

[19] Douglas Young, *'Plastic Scots' and the Scottish Literary Tradition* (William McLellan, Glasgow, 1946), pp. 22–23.

Gorgons frae Crail sall sune jurmummle. Wow!
I'll pit my best fuit forrit nou tae fesh them.[20]

Here the literary Scots blends familiar language such as 'skellum'
(meaning 'rascal') and 'thrapple' ('throat') with occasionally rare and
archaic vocabulary, such as 'harigals' (a southern Scots word, meaning
'intestines') and compounds such as 'bluid-drippan' ('blood-dripping')
and 'whin-hertit' ('stony-hearted'). Contemporary phrasing is evident
in Dionysus's 'teuch guy' and Aiakos's 'pit my best fuit forrit [forward]',
and there are obvious allusions which domesticate the Greek: the
reference to Cerberus as a 'collie', to the East Neuk fishing village of
Crail (near St Andrews, where the translation was first performed),
and, most obviously, to the Loch Ness monster, which, Young's notes
inform us, is a rendition of the Greek for 'Tartessos's conger-eel'.

Young's debt to Douglas, both in choice of text and strategy of
translation, however qualified, is clear, but perhaps the most obvious
act of homage to the medieval makar is the selection of *Tales frae the
Odyssey o Homer, Owerset intil Scots* by William Neill. Neill's purpose
in translating Homer into Scots strongly echoes Douglas's:

> The aim o this buik wes tae mak sic a tellin o a gret tale as wad gae
> ower eithlie [easily] intil Scots an tae gie a heize tae the hairts o thir
> fowk wha still tak pleisure in the auld an nobil tung.[21]

Again, there is the appeal to the noble tradition of literature in Scots,
and the implication that Scots is the language which lifts the hearts of
folk – although here these people are acknowledged to be a diminishing group. Neill argues for the authenticity of his variety of Scots,
but his verse shows several of the characteristics recommended by
Young, above. In this excerpt, Ulysess is answering the Cyclops,
Polyphemous's, interrogation about the whereabouts of his ship:

> 'Yird-duntin Poseidon dinged ma ship tae skelfs
> an coost her wi the laundbrist on yir coast,
> twes he that brocht her in ablo the mull

---

[20] Aristophanes and Douglas Young, *The Puddocks*, 2nd edition (Makarsbield,
Fife, 1958), p. 16, lines 463–78.
[21] William Neill, *Tales frae the Odyssey o Homer* (Saltire Society, Edinburgh,
1992), p. 10.

an the wund drave her in frae the sea
but I wi thir men joukit a sair weird.'[22]

Again we see the familiar Scots vocabulary, such as 'skelfs' ('splinters')
mixing with rarer vocabulary, such as 'laundbrist' ('waves breaking on
shore'; a term recorded in Caithness until the early twentieth century),
and archaisms such as 'weird' ('fate', as in Shakespeare's 'weird sisters').
Again, it is illuminating to compare Neill's literary Scots with an
English translation, such as E.V. Rieu and D.C.H. Rieu's prose version:

'As for my ship, it was wrecked by the Earthshaker Poseidon on the
borders of your land. The wind had carried us on to a lee shore. He
drove the ship up to a headland and hurled it on the rocks. But I and
my friends here managed to escape with our lives.'[23]

The modern translations of Blok, Aristophanes and Homer into literary
Scots send a complex set of sometimes contradictory signals which their
English counterparts obviously do not do. Standard English, through
the process of becoming a non-regional, fully-functioning official language of a heterogenous, multinational state, has been largely deraci-
nated; Scots, having avoided the process of standardisation, has the
potential to speak to and for a more particular speech community.
Neill's version of Homer is still an act of nationalism in the way that
Rieu and Rieu's translation is not. A paradox of such translations as
Neill's is that this act of linguistic nationalism results in a translation
which even many Scots, as the translator acknowledges, will find
difficult to understand, at least at first sight.

Translations into literary Scots perhaps embody best the contradictions of Lallans writing. They appeal to history, but use a language that
is in many respects new: a recreated rather than a revived Scots. They
look outwards to the world, but principally to raise the status of the
home nation and one of its forms of communication. The appeal of the
variety of Scots used is that it is 'the language of the people', but that
language is such a synthesis of fading regionalisms, neologisms, archaisms and borrowings that many, if not most, of 'the people' struggle to
comprehend it.

Even if it is at times difficult to understand, literary Scots is not

---

[22] Neill (ibid.), pp. 35–36.
[23] E.V. Rieu and D.C.H. Rieu, trans., *Homer: The Odyssey* (Penguin, Harmondsworth, 1991), p. 132; bk 9, lines 284–87.

necessarily unpopular. The greatest translation into Scots of the twentieth century was also one of the country's most surprising publishing
successes of recent decades: financed largely by public subscription,
William Lorimer's New Testament in Scots sold two and a half thousand
copies in hardback, within a fortnight of its appearance in 1983.[24] This
was not the first Scots Bible, but it is undeniably the most impressive.
A Greek scholar, Lorimer went back to the Aramaic texts as the source
of his translation, and his version of the New Testament reflects his
profound knowledge of both the source language and of the expressive
capability of Scots. An illustration of Lorimer's style can be given by
comparing a passage from the Authorised Version with the Scots New
Testament (Mark, I. 14–17):

Now after that, John was put in prison, Jesus came into Galilee,
preaching the gospel of the kingdom of God. And saying, The time
is fulfilled, and the kingdom of God is at hand: repent ye, and believe
the gospel.
Now as he walked by the sea of Galilee, he saw Simon and Andrew
his brother casting a net into the sea: for they were fishers. And Jesus
said unto them, Come ye after me, and I will make you fishers of men.
And straightway they forsook their nets, and followed him.

Eftir John hed been incarcerate, Jesus fuir tae Galilee an there
preached the Gospel o God. 'The time hes comed,' he said, 'an the
Kingdom o God is naurhand: repent ye, an believe i the Gospel.'
    Ae day he wis gaein alangside the Loch o Galilee, whan he saw
Simon an his brither Andro castin their net i the watter – they war
fishers tae tredd – an he said til them, 'Come awà eftir me, an I's mak
ye men-fishers'; an strecht they quat their nets an fallowt him.[25]

Lorimer shares his fellow-translators' concern to raise the profile of
Scots, and to demonstrate its expressive potential. The very choice of
the Bible as a source text has cultural implications, since the decline of
Scots has been widely perceived as being partly caused by the enormous
social influence of the Authorised Version on reformed Scotland. More
than the other Lallans translations, therefore, Lorimer's text has been

24 Graham Tulloch, A History of the Scots Bible (Aberdeen University Press,
Aberdeen, 1989), pp. 72–83 contains a discussion of the text and its production.
25 W.L. Lorimer, trans., The New Testament in Scots (Southside Publishers,
Edinburgh, 1983), p. 61.

adopted by supporters of the project to standardise the Scots language. Tulloch, for example, makes much of Lorimer's achievement in utilising a 'standard' Scots:

> Scots can itself be seen as a standard language, an alternative standard to Standard English but one which follows in many cases the usages of everyday speech. Similarly New Testament Greek had its own standard, departing from standard literary Greek towards the popular spoken language. In this sense, Scots offers the opportunity to use a standard language with a high input from popular speech as the medium for translating another standard language strongly influenced by everyday spoken usage.[26]

Tulloch's claims here echo the paradoxes and contradictions we have already seen in the discussion of translations into Scots. Lorimer's New Testament is obviously a gift to those who wish to promote a standard Scots which is equivalent to standard English. The process of standardisation involves status-raising, corpus-building and acquisition-planning,[27] and the availability of an 'authoritative', if not authorised, version of the sacred text of the dominant culture is a key strategy in this process. The status of Scots is raised by Lorimer's scholarly translation; it may provide a model for further writing in Scots; and it is a text which is eminently suitable for use in kirk and school. Lorimer's New Testament, however, does not provide a simple or homogeneous model for further writing in Scots: again a literary construction rather than an 'authentic' rendering of Scottish speech, Lorimer's New Testament is written in a variety of 'dialects' based loosely on the regional varieties of present-day Scots. The rationale for this is given in Lorimer's notebooks, prepared for his son, Robert, who assisted him in his later years and prepared the text for publication after his death. They show that Lorimer believed that 'Jesus spakna Standard Aramaic – for ordnar oniegate – but guid ("braid") Galilee, an the New Testament isna written in Standard Greek, as the Kirk Faithers alloued.'[28] Lorimer, then, varied the Scots that he used – dividing the New Testament into

---

[26] Tulloch (op. cit.), p. 76.
[27] See, for example, Robert L. Cooper, *Language Planning and Social Change* (Cambridge University Press, Cambridge 1989); and, from a Scots perspective, J. Derrick McClure, A.J. Aitken, and John Thomas Low, *The Scots Language: Planning for Modern Usage* (The Ramsay Head Press, Edinburgh, 1980).
[28] Tulloch (op. cit.), p. 75.

twelve sections which he assumed were composed by different authors, and attempting to be internally consistent within these sections. In doing so, Lorimer 's translation adds a further contradiction to those suggested above: the authority of his translation partly derives from his use of a range of equivalent varieties of Scots, varieties whose very equivalence derives from the absence of a standard Scots. This range reflects the patchwork of dialects found in the source text. However, the authority of this translation is then used by others to further the process of standardising Scots.

There are, of course, writers and translators who reject the creation of a standard Scots, and who see the literary variety of Scots, Lallans, as an 'artificial' variety which robs Scots of its power to represent the people. Such a rejection is vividly expressed by Malcolm Youngson, whose antipathy to the practice of resurrecting archaisms is distilled into his dislike of the use of the word 'aiblins' ('perhaps'), often used by Lallans writers:

> Those who feel that a pure English does not wholly encompass the Scottish experience as mediated through language may by all means introduce a peculiarly Scottish word, if the situation calls for it in their judgement. Those who feel impelled to write in dialect are equally entitled to do so. But let us cast aside this falsification – for such it is – that a reconstructed Scots is feasible or, indeed desirable . . . A final word: as I said, nobody hears anyone speak of 'aiblins' nowadays. How would it be if a poet writing in English introduced terms such as 'doth' or 'mayhap' or 'verily' into his verse? He would probably be laughed out of court and his poems would find it hard to gain a place in any literary magazine. Why, then, must we have 'aiblins' and 'maun' and such-like inflicted upon us? Let the dead bury the dead.[29]

Those translators who do not participate in the tradition of reconstructing a literary Scots, a tradition which, as we have seen, extends from the sixteenth to the twentieth century, tend to adopt a mode of speech which is closer to the regional and social varieties of today's Scotland. However, these writers can be seen as treading common ground with the 'Lallans' writers: if their chosen medium is indeed closer to 'the language of the people', its status is nevertheless raised above that of regional literature by the long tradition of writing in Scots, for a

[29] Malcolm Youngson, *Chapman* 69–70 (Autumn, 1992), p. 92.

Scottish nation. Liz Lochhead's translation of Molière's *Tartuffe* falls into this category, as does Edwin Morgan's recent critically successful and popular adaptation of Rostand's *Cyrano de Bergerac*. Morgan's translation of *Cyrano* into Glaswegian Scots bears close scrutiny. One of the outstanding poets of his generation, Morgan is equally at home when writing English and Scots, as well as concrete and sound poems. His choice of Glaswegian for *Cyrano* can be seen as an act of civic pride as much as cultural nationalism. As he says himself in the Introduction:

> Various English versions of the play have been made, but it is one of those rich and challenging works which need to be translated again and again, in different circumstances and for different purposes, readerly and actorly. The time seemed ripe for a Scottish version, but one that would be thoroughly stageworthy, and not incomprehensible to audiences at the Edinburgh International Festival. I decided that an urban Glaswegian Scots would offer the best basis, since it is widely spoken, can accommodate contemporary reference, is by no means incapable of the lyrical and the poetic, and comes unburdened by the baggage of the older Scots which used to be thought suitable for historical plays.[30]

The avoidance of the 'baggage of the older Scots' might be seen as an implicit acknowledgement that Lallans's claim to be the language of the people is a flawed one, particularly as we approach the end of the century, when even passive knowledge of traditional Scots is declining. It should not necessarily be read as a rejection of the use of Lallans wholesale, since Morgan elsewhere writes poetry (including translations of Mayakovsky) in a more 'literary' Scots. And there are some correspondences between Morgan's Glaswegian idiom and Young's literary Scots – both take inventive delight in 'flyting', that is, the practice of ritualised insult which can be traced back to the court of James IV: as we have seen, the whole Scottish tradition of translation begins with Douglas flyting Caxton. The passage from *The Puddocks* continues this tradition, as does the wonderful scene in *Cyrano de Bergerac* in which Cyrano demonstrates how others (if they dared) could most expressively describe his nose:

[30] Edwin Morgan, trans., *Edmond Rostand's Cyrano de Bergerac* (Carcanet, Manchester, 1992), p. xi.

CYRANO: Yer *canto'* s no *bel*, young man!
Ye could have said – oh, lotsa things, a plan
For each, tae suit yer tone o voice, like so:
Thuggish: 'If Ah'd a nose like yours, Ah'd go
Straight to the surgery fur amputation!'
Freen-like: 'Dinnae dunk it in a cup, fashion
Yersel a Munich tankard for tae slurp fae.'
Descriptive: 'A rock? A peak? A cape? The survey
Shaws the cape's a haill peninsula!'
Pawky: 'If it's a boax and no a fistula,
Whit's in it, pen's or pins or penny needles?'
Gracious: 'Ye're a right Saint Francis, ye wheedle
The burds o the air tae wrap their gentle tootsies
Roon yer perch an rest their weary Guccis!'
Truculent: 'Puff yer pipe until the smoke
Comes whummlin oot yer nose, and the big toke
Has awe yer neebors cryin "Lum's on fire!"' [31]

Compare this version with one of the more interesting of the 'various English versions' of the play, Jatinda Verma and Ranjit Bolt's 'tradaptation' of the play to the India of the 1930s:

CYRANO: That's it? Just long?
My friend, I'm not at all impressed: among
The myriad taunts you might have hit upon
You come up with that pathetic one.
'Long!' Not exactly wounding, is it? Why,
There are countless angles you could try;
Aggressive, for example – you could jeer:
'Amputation might be an idea.
It's an absurd proboscis!' Or again,
Mischievous: 'May I shelter from the rain
Under that . . . thing?'
Or curious: 'What is that?
A peg on which you hang your coat and hat?
A babu's desk?' Or venomously twee:
'You really love our feathered friends, I see.
You carry round a whatsit where they rest
Their dainty little feet, or even nest.'

31 Morgan (ibid.), p. 24; Act 1, Scene 4.

Snide: 'Your nose, dost, is beyond a joke.
It must look like a chimney when you smoke!'[32]

In Scots, usually, the 'jeer/idea' rhyme would not work; still, there are many interesting points of comparison between the two texts. The Indian provenance of the latter is here suggested mainly by lexical items, 'babu' and 'dost', although elsewhere the text switches into Indian languages, the corporate whole being referred to by Verma as 'Binglish'.[33] The Scots text is denser, indicating pronunciations which are particularly Glaswegian (the first person pronoun, 'Ah'), as well as incorporating traditional features of Scots grammar (including the infinitive 'for tae slurp') and vocabulary ('lum' meaning 'chimney'). Linguistically, the Scots text is much more rooted in Glasgow than the Indian text is rooted in the Calcutta of the Raj. Even so, the Scots is not nearly so dense as that we have seen in other translations discussed in this paper. The character of Cyrano cries out for translations into language varieties which situate themselves in opposition to standard English: a provincial Gascon in Paris, Cyrano personifies the clash between the cultures of the so-called margins and the dominant culture of the perceived centre. Cyrano is a heroic figure, but his long nose denies him due recognition, and the confidence to court Roxanne. His comedy and tragedy are powerful, romantic metaphors for those brilliant cultures which are tainted by the stigma of parochialism.

Present-day Scots, then, offers translators not one but a range of varieties which exist outwith the orbit of standard English, which have a complex but powerful set of historical and cultural associations, and which may be particulary appropriate for the rendition of texts which focus on questions of cultural marginality. Bill Findlay and Martin Bowman's translations of the plays of Michel Tremblay, particularly *The House Among the Stars* (*La Maison Suspendue*), provide the most economical support for this claim. Tremblay's wonderful plays of Québécois life sit on the margins of Canadian culture; the language of the source texts is itself usually non-standard Québécois French, the low-status 'Joual' which means, literarally, 'horse language'. In *La Maison Suspendue*, however, Tremblay distinguishes between three generations of a family, partly by varying the dialect of Québécois French spoken by each generation. In their translation of the play as *The House Among*

---

[32] Jatinda Verma and Ranjit Bolt, trans., *Cyrano, Edmond Rostand* (Absolute Classics, Bath, 1995), p. 28; Act 1. The term 'tradaptation' is their own.
[33] Verma and Bolt (op. cit.), p. 6.

the Stars, Bowman and Findlay leapt at the opportunity to use different
varieties of Scots to parallel the dialectal shifts in the source text. As
the translators themselves acknowledge:

> in the final analysis the key attraction [in translating the play] was
> our confidence that Scots would prove an especially effective trans-
> lation medium, allowing us to get closer in letter and spirit to
> Tremblay's Montreal Québécois than would prove possible using
> English.[34]

The resulting translation exploits the full range of possibilities open to
today's translators into Scots.[35] The language of the oldest generation,
a brother and sister living in a rural homestead in 1910, is based on a
traditional Scots, which leans towards Lallans in its, at times, poetic or
'literary' qualities. The language of the middle generation, returning to
the house in 1950, is an urban vernacular, closer to the Scots of
Morgan's *Cyrano de Bergerac*. The youngest generation, again returning
to the house in 1990, speaks standard Scottish English: a dialect which
in its few but distinct Scottish markers is roughly comparable to the
'Binglish' extract from the Indian version of *Cyrano* discussed above.
The three generations, in their own time-frame, are presented on-stage
simultaneously. The following excerpt gives a brief flavour of the play.
Edouard and the Fat Woman belong to the middle generation; Mathieu
belongs to the youngest generation, and Josaphat to the oldest:

EDOUARD: Ah think we'd better go intae the hoose . . .
THE FAT WOMAN: The mosquitoes arenae oot yit, ah'm gaun-
nae sit oan the verandah.
EDOUARD: Yir right. It's owre early fur bed yit. Ah'll go'n see if
ah kin coax Bartine tae jine us.
THE FAT WOMAN: Light mair lamps when yir in . . . This hoose
is sad-like right enough when thurs nae lights in it at night-time . . .

---

34 Martin Bowman and Bill Findlay, 'Québécois into Scots: Translating
Michel Tremblay', *Scottish Language* no. 13 (1994), p. 66. The translation, *The
House Among the Stars*, is presently unpublished, but can be accessed on
the World Wide Web, as one of a number of Scots texts gathered
by the COMET project, based at Glasgow University. The web site is
http://www.arts.gla.ac.uk./www/english/comet/comet.html
35 See John Corbett 'COMET and *The House Among the Stars*', in *The Glasgow
Review* no. 4 (1996), pp. 89–103 for a detailed discussion of the Scots variety
used by each generation.

EDOUARD: *(In a falsetto voice)* Bartine? It's me, your sister-in-law back again . . . You and me's going to have a wee chinwag . . . You know how much you enjoy that!
   Silence.
   Josaphat lights his pipe.
THE FAT WOMAN: Ye kin smell the water fae up here.
MATHIEU: It's funny, isn't it? I can't smell the trees and the water anymore. When we arrived it was fresh and strong. Two hours later it's gone. It makes you want to go away so's you can come back and smell it again.
   The Fat Woman and Mathieu take a deep breath.
JOSAPHAT: The smell ae ma pipe tobaccie 'll bring Victoire oot
. . .
(He turns towards the house.) Ah need tae hiv a talk wi you.
THE FAT WOMAN: *(Rather loud.)* Are yese comin oot?
MATHIEU: It gives me a funny feeling listening to you tell your family's stories . . .

In this play, the history of the family – its move from country to city, and from peasantry to working-class to middle-class – has a dramatic index in the history of the language varieties used. The use of a traditional, near-literary variety for the oldest generation imbues that part of the translation with a poetic nostalgia; the use of a broad urban vernacular for the middle-generation adds to the comedic associations of that part of the text; while the use of a near-standard Scots for the youngest generation expresses vividly the sense of rootlessness which draws them back to the family house.

In their textbook on translation, Hatim and Mason urge novice translators to be aware of the geographical, social and political implications of the use of any language variety:

> We recall the controversy in Scotland a few years ago over the use of Scottish accents in representing the speech of Russian peasants in the TV dramatisation of a foreign play. The inference was allowed that a Scottish accent might somehow be associated with low status, something which, no doubt, was not intended. Like producers and directors, translators have to be constantly alert to the social implications of their decisions.[36]

---

[36] Basil Hatim and Ian Mason, *Discourse and the Translator* (Longman, London and New York, 1990), p. 40.

As this paper has, I hope, demonstrated, such protests about the pigeon-holing of Scots speech as a single, homogeneous, regional variety of English, with simple values and associations, are justified – or, at least, they are not only the product of the Scots' notorious sensitivity about others hijacking our national image. Translations into Scots must be considered in terms of a Scottish tradition, independent of English tradition, but obviously related to it insofar as it is, at times, oppositional. Translations into Scots exploit a complex range of language varieties, and they do so, at times, to express a proud and long-standing cultural independence; and, at other times, to express and share the lively complexities of those cultures which, in metropolitan terms, might be placed at the margins.

Marian Evans, the Translator

SUSANNE STARK

WHEN GEORGE ELIOT DIED a widely acclaimed novelist in 1881, a number of her contemporaries paid instant tribute to the significance of her literary achievements in obituaries and biographies of book length. Many of them devoted considerable attention to the period of the author's life before she wrote novels under a male pseudonym. Prior to the serialization of the *Scenes of Clerical Life* in *Blackwood's Magazine* in 1857 Marian Evans published anonymous periodical articles as well as two major translations from the German. While she made every possible effort to avoid being associated with the 1846 English rendering of David Friedrich Strauss' *Das Leben Jesu* (1835), her 1854 translation of Ludwig Feuerbach's *Das Wesen des Christentums* (1841) is significantly the only book in which the author's real name, Marian Evans, appeared in print (Cross 1884, I, 263).[1] The author of the obituary note in *Blackwood's Magazine* came to the conclusion that George Eliot actively sought to avoid connecting 'these books or her contributions to the "Westminster Review" with the great name by which the world knew her' (Allardyce 1881, 258). Similarly, Leslie Stephen in an unsigned obituary article in the *Cornhill* raised the question as to why George Eliot did not 'write immortal works in her youth, instead of translating German authors of a heterodox tendency', but eventually came to the following conclusion:

> Certainly, I do not think that any one who has had a little experience in such matters would regard it as otherwise than dangerous for a powerful mind to be precipitated into public utterance. The Pythagorean probation of silence may be protracted too long; but it may afford a most useful discipline: and I think that there is nothing preposterous in the supposition that George Eliot's work was all the

Acknowledgement: I am grateful to Dr Helen Chambers for her advice and encouragement.
1 Interestingly enough, this fact is not reflected in the 1957 reprint of the Feuerbach translation, which attributes the translation to George Eliot as opposed to Marian Evans.

more powerful because it came from a novelist who had lain fallow
through a longer period than ordinary. (Stephen 1881, 466–67)

What, then, were the moving forces behind this supposedly mute,
silent and fallow period in which George Eliot was still Marian Evans,
and what was the nature of her motives for primarily engaging in
contributions to the *Westminster Review*, as well as published and
unpublished translation projects? It is frequently disregarded that, apart
from the two German theological works mentioned in the obituary
notices, Marian Evans also considered translating *Mémoire en faveur de
la liberté des Cultes* (1826) by the Swiss theologian Alexandre Rodolphe
Vinet from the French and actually rendered Spinoza's *Tractatus
Theologico-Politicus* (1670) as well as his *Ethics* (1677) from Latin into
English.[2] In addition, she was the 'accomplished German translator'
acknowledged in a footnote, who contributed anonymously to George
Henry Lewes' *Life of Goethe* (1855) (Lewes 1968, 328; Haight 1968,
172–73). Henry James, one of reviewers of the 1884 biography of
George Eliot by J.W. Cross, which aimed at creating authenticity by
publishing a wide range of extracts from the author's letters and journals, drew his readers' attention to the fact that in her twenties Marian
Evans still considered it to be 'ungodly to go to concerts and to read
novels' (James 1885, 492; see also Cross 1884, I, 42; GE *Letters*, I, 23).
This attitude also accounts for the fact that she initially shrank from
undertaking creative writing. Even when she had succeeded in over-
coming this inhibition in her own life, she never forgot her initial
reluctance and did not lose her sympathy for other women who were
less courageous than her (GE *Letters*, III, 44). On a more theoretical
level she looked for scientific reasons why English and German women
did not have the same intellectual capacity as French women to
establish a considerable female literary tradition. In attempting to find
an answer to this question she came up with the following explanation
in an essay entitled 'Woman in France: Madame de Sablé':

---

[2] The Vinet translation, first mentioned in 1842 (*The Letters of George Eliot*,
ed. by G. S. Haight, I, 135), did not actually materialize (GE *Letters*, I,
157–58). The *Tractatus* translation mentioned in her correspondence in the
years 1843 (GE *Letters*, I, 158) and 1849 (GE *Letters*, I, 280–81) has never
been found, and neither of the Spinoza translations were published during
George Eliot's lifetime. Her rendering of the *Ethics* was eventually printed in
1981.

The primary one (i.e. reason), perhaps, lies in the physiological characteristics of the Gallic race: the small brain and vivacious temperament which permit the fragile system of woman to sustain the superlative activity requisite for intellectual creativeness; while, on the other hand, the larger brain and slower temperament of the English and Germans are, in the womanly organization, generally dreamy and passive.... The woman of large capacity can seldom rise beyond the absorption of ideas; her physical conditions refuse to support the energy required for spontaneous activity; the voltaic-pile is not strong enough to produce crystallizations; phantasms of great ideas float through her mind, but she has not the spell which will arrest them, and give them fixity. This, more than unfavourable external circumstance, is, we think, the reason why woman has not yet contributed any new form to art, any discovery in science, any deep-searching inquiry in philosophy. (GE 1854, 55–56)

This statement was published in 1854 only three years before Marian Evans adopted a male pseudonym and published her first piece of fiction. The passage is, however, in many ways the attempt to provide a scientific justification for the 'Pythagorean silence' with which Marian Evans started her own literary career. An earlier, less sophisticated, though far more amusing, reflection of her own role can be found in an undeservedly ignored document. Only Mathilde Blind, the first biographer of George Eliot, appears to have had access to a letter written by Marian Evans to an intimate friend soon after the completion of the Strauss translation in 1846.[3] Despite all scientific evidence for the lack of creativity in Englishwomen referred to above, it can hardly be claimed that the letter mentioned in Blind's biography is deficient in imaginative spontaneity:

Miss Evans pretends that, to her gratification, she has actually had a visit from a real live German professor, whose musty person was encased in a still mustier coat. This learned personage has come over to England with the single purpose of getting his voluminous writings translated into English. There are at least twenty volumes, all unpublished, owing to the envious machinations of rival authors, none of them treating of anything more modern than Cheops, or the invention of the hieroglyphics. The respectable professor's object in

[3] Mathilde Blind (1841–1896) also followed in George Eliot's footsteps in that she provided the 1873 English rendering of Strauss' *The Old Faith and the New* only one year after the work had been published in German.

coming to England is to secure a wife and translator in one. But though, on inquiry, he finds that the ladies engaged in translation are legion, they mostly turn out to be utterly incompetent, besides not answering to his requirements in other respects; the qualifications he looks for in a wife, besides a thorough acquaintance with English and German, being personal ugliness and a snug little capital, sufficient to supply him with a moderate allowance of tobacco and *Schwarzbier*, after defraying the expense of printing his books. To find this phoenix among women he is sent to Coventry on all hands.

(Blind 1883, 46)

While the author of this letter in many ways foreshadows the novelist George Eliot, the fictional translatress, undoubtedly an ironic self-portrayal of Marian Evans, is doomed to become the wife of this unattractive and dull German professor and does not get the chance to engage in creative writing and an independent career as an author in her own right.

Marian Evans' translation of Strauss in real life in many respects reflects the ambivalence of this letter. For the English rendering of Strauss' work was suggested by a circle of Coventry free-thinkers, widely associated with three families: the Brays, the Hennells and the Brabants. Her decision to translate Strauss was thus not an active, self-initiated one, but the result of her social connections with these families. Marian Evans' departure from her own strict evangelical upbringing, her disagreement with her father about religious matters and her involvement in the rationalist circles of Coventry in the early 1840s has been widely and meticulously documented. Who, then, urged Marian Evans to translate David Friedrich Strauss' *Das Leben Jesu*, and why was there a sense that German biblical criticism deserved to be disseminated in England? Strauss fell on fertile ground in Coventry, for under the influence of the rationalist tendencies of Charles Bray, author of various philosophical and educational works, his brother-in-law, Charles Hennell, had already undertaken a critical examination of the New Testament narratives. The result of these studies was the publication of *An Inquiry Concerning the Origin of Christianity* in 1838. Before then Charles Hennell had indeed not read Strauss' *Das Leben Jesu*, which first came out in Germany in 1835. A translation of the work was first suggested in the house of the Benthamite Liberal Joseph Parkes. He and his friends also raised the funds necessary to convince John Chapman to proceed with the publication of the work. Charles Hennell took it upon himself to find a suitable translator and won Dr Brabant's daughter Rufa, his future wife, for the project. Until their wedding in 1843 she was in charge of the translation and rendered a considerable amount of the first volume of the work's fourth edition from German into English. As a married woman, however, she no longer wished to continue her literary work and was reassured by her sister-in-law, Sara Hennell, that Marian Evans was perfectly qualified to take over the task (GE *Letters*, I, 171). In addition, Sara Hennell was willing to assist Marian Evans in her efforts. Her competent academic and linguistic judgement, as well as her help with proof-reading, are amply documented in George Eliot's correspondence.

In order to evaluate Marian Evans' involvement in the translation of the *Life of Jesus* a variety of questions need to be addressed: what were her motives for engaging in the English rendering of a controversial German theological treatise, which took her over two years and thus demanded more time and mental energy than most of her novels? To what extent was the project simply imposed on her because of the need to replace a woman who found it impossible to combine literary activity with married life? Did her reluctance to see her name connected with the translation suggest she was merely a mute and passive mediator without opinion and judgment of her own, or did she have a vested interest in Strauss' ideas? In other words, was she predestined by her own *physique*, the large brain and weak voltaic pile of an Englishwoman, which allowed her to absorb ideas but denied her the power to create, or was the translation of Strauss' text a cautious expression of her own convictions and the beginning of a period of original literary creation?

Without doubt the task of rendering Strauss' *Das Leben Jesu* into English made great demands on her ability to absorb both languages and ideas. During her lifetime George Eliot acquired a comprehensive literary and scholarly knowledge of four modern languages: French, German, Italian and Spanish (Cross 1884, III, 372). In addition, ample evidence for her competence in dealing with Latin can be found in her two Spinoza translations. Frequently overlooked in connection with the Strauss rendering, however, is the fact that it was not merely an exercise in grappling with extremely complex German theological terminology but that it also required a sound grasp of Hebrew, Greek and Latin. For unlike Marian Evans, who provided English renderings of Greek quotations if their meaning did not become clear from the text, Strauss did not offer this service to the readers of his original German text (GE *Letters*, I, 199). Quite possibly her motive for taking these pains was, as she admitted in a conversation with Oscar Browning, one of her later biographers, that she could never 'understand anything of a Greek writer' until she had 'come to comprehend every word'

(Browning 1890, 26). In addition, Cross recorded that Hebrew was one of her favourite subjects throughout her life, and even though she did not possess her own dictionary when she worked on *Das Leben Jesu* she committed herself to rendering all Hebrew words into English (Cross 1884, III, 372; *GE Letters*, I, 203–04). Strauss' treatise in English translation was thus converted into a more readable piece of scholarship than the German text had ever been.

Marian Evans' thorough work was highly acclaimed in the contemporary periodical press. The article on Strauss' *Life of Jesus* in the *Prospective Review*, for example, begins in the following manner:

> At length the far-famed Leben Jesu of Strauss appears before the English Public in a fitting shape – in a faithful, elegant and scholarlike translation, and a clear and readable type. . . . Whoever reads these volumes without any reference to the German, must be pleased with the easy, perspicuous, idiomatic and harmonious force of the English style. But he will be still more satisfied when on turning to the original, he finds that the rendering is word for word, thought for thought, and sentence for sentence. . . . But in preparing so beautiful a rendering as the present, the difficulties can have been neither few nor small in the way of preserving, in various parts of the work, the exactness of the translation, combined with that uniform harmony and clearness of style, which impart to the volumes before us the air and spirit of an original. (Anon. 1846a, 479)

As these observations show, the reviewer generously acknowledged the pivotal role the translator played in the reception of Strauss' work in England. The necessary capacity for the absorption of a complex piece of scholarship in a foreign language referred to above did not only manifest itself in linguistic accuracy. All the reviewers who paid attention to the quality of the translation were convinced that the person in charge of it must have been intimately acquainted with the theological and philosophical background to Strauss' treatise. This expertise was, however, associated with a masculine intellect, and none of the reviewers supposed that a woman was responsible for the translation. The author of the *Prospective Review* article observed and suspected that despite the fact that 'the translator never obtrudes himself upon the reader with any notes or comments of his own, he is evidently a man who has a familiar knowledge of the whole subject' (Ibid.). Other periodicals like the *British Quarterly Review* shared the assumption that the translator of Strauss was male (Alexander 1847, 206). Marian Evans herself obviously agreed with this gender perception at that time because in an 1844 letter to Mrs Bray she disapproved of the fact that Strauss had been told that a young lady was translating his book. She was concerned that 'he must have some twinges of alarm to think he was dependent on that most contemptible specimen of the human being for his English reputation' (GE *Letters*, I, 177).

In addition, concern was expressed about the fact that the translator is necessarily to a certain extent associated with the contents of the work. In this context it was suggested that 'the translator might have employed his talents to much better purpose' and that England 'could have done quite as well' without Strauss (Alexander 1847, 206). This statement raises the question why Strauss' work caused such strong feelings of opposition and to what extent Marian Evans agreed with the author. There can be no doubt that the first German edition of *Das Leben Jesu* in 1835 provoked a widespread sensation by questioning orthodox religious beliefs and it led to Strauss' dismissal from the theological seminary at the University of Tübingen, where he had served as a lecturer (Harris 1973, 58–65).[4] The author subsequently made considerable concessions to his critics in the third and fourth editions of the work (Strauss 1973, XXXVI–XXXVIII). Nevertheless, it continued to convey a revolutionary explosiveness which is closely linked to the problem of translation, for the main object of his study was to resolve the question as to how the language, the form and the content of New Testament stories, which frequently lack all scientific probability, can best be 'translated' into the language of his own day. In the preface to the first edition Strauss defined his own approach in the following manner:

It appeared to the author of the work, the first half of which is herewith submitted to the public, that it was time to substitute a new mode of considering the life of Jesus, in the place of the antiquated systems of supranaturalism and naturalism. . . . The new point of view, which must take the place of the above, is the mythical.

(Strauss 1846, I, IX)

---

[4] In 1839 Strauss was also debarred from a professorship in Zürich which he had been invited to assume. His retirement from academic theological circles, which lasted more than twenty years, was spent in Germany. In his last work, *The Old Faith and the New*, he replaced Christianity with a Darwinistic scientific materialism.

Strauss' mythical view repudiated both the historicity and the supranaturalism of the biblical stories. Despite that, he did not perceive
his method to be a threat to the Christian faith:

> The supernatural birth of Christ, his miracles, his resurrection and
> ascension, remain eternal truths, whatever doubts may be cast on
> their reality as historical facts. . . . A dissertation at the close of the
> work will show that the dogmatic significance of the life of Jesus
> remains inviolate: in the mean time let the calmness and insensibility
> with which, in the course of it, criticism undertakes apparently
> dangerous operations, be explained solely by the security of the
> author's conviction that no injury is threatened to the Christian
> faith. (Ibid., XI)

Significantly, Marian Evans decided on 'insensibility' for rendering
the German 'Kaltblütigkeit' even though in retrospect, after her translation had gone into print, she preferred the exact equivalent of 'sang
froid' or 'coldbloodedness' (GE Letters, I, 217). The decision-making
process recorded here is indicative of the careful precision with which
she treated the translation and is, like many other questions concerning
the rendering of the German text, documented meticulously in her
correspondence. In the case of 'Kaltblütigkeit', the option of 'coldbloodedness' as opposed to 'insensibility' in English would have conveyed the negative and destructive overtones the German term
undoubtedly invokes. German biblical criticism was, after all, in England widely associated with a scrutinizing academic rigour and was
considered to place German scholars ahead of their English colleagues
in this field (GE 1851, 30). A stimulating way of explaining the
differences in biblical scholarship in England and Germany has been
suggested by Stephen Prickett:

> Because of the comparative lack of development of prose narrative
> and any accompanying critical theory in Germany at the end of the
> eighteenth century it was natural for the new wave of German critical
> scholars to think of the biblical narratives in 'poetic', anthropologi-
> cal, and mythological terms, rather than in ways drawn from the
> novel and prose narrative. This was as true, moreover, for those
> interested in the literary structure of the Bible as it was for the
> historical critics. (Prickett 1991, 190)

It is precisely to this form of scholarship that Marian Evans with all her
initial hesitations about the reading and writing of novels turned.

As we have already noted above, however, many English reviewers saw Strauss' achievements in a very critical light. Generally speaking he was considered to be one of those German scholars who 'turns human nature into a steam-engine, and supposes that we may interpret its movements by some uniform law' (Anon. 1846a, 507). In 1855 Marian Evans herself described these intellectuals as 'spinners of elaborate cocoons – German system-mongers' (GE 1855, 149). Strauss made use of philological scholarship in order to examine the credibility of the New Testament. This method was perceived to be intrinsically German and had previously been discussed and questioned in England in the reception of German historical writing. Even then critics were concerned about the implications for their religious faith if the 'coldblooded' method of dissecting a written source were applied to biblical texts. (Blind 1883, 39) The article in the British Quarterly Review goes as far as to compare Strauss' scrutiny of his sources and his attempt to establish the true story of the life of Jesus with a court case in which witnesses are called to give evidence in order to distinguish between natural and supranatural elements, between fact and fiction in biblical accounts, so that the judge of the case can draw up a new mythical interpretation of the story. The reviewer also drew his readers' attention to major faults in Strauss' research, which derived in part from serious mistakes Strauss had made in his own translation from ancient sources (Alexander 1847, 215–16).

Marian Evans' attitude towards Strauss was ambivalent. It is reported that in 1844 the translator worked away speedily and managed to get through six pages per day. In a letter to Sara Hennell she wrote the following about her attitude to the project:

> Thank you for the encouragement you sent me – I only need it when my head is weak and I am unable to do much. Then I sicken at the idea of having Strauss in my head and on my hands for a lustrum, instead of saying good bye to him in a year. When I can work fast I am never weary, nor do I regret either that the work has been begun, or that I have undertaken it. I am only inclined to vow that I will never translate again if I live to correct the sheets for Strauss.
>
> (GE Letters, I, 176)

It is probably the scholarly ruthlessness of the author's method which made Marian Evans 'Strauss-sick' towards the end of her project. In 1846 Mrs Charles Bray observed in a letter to Sara Sophia Hennell that 'it made her ill dissecting the beautiful story of the crucifixion, and only the sight of her Christ-image and picture made her endure it' (*GE Letters*, I, 206). The following passage from Strauss' account will serve to exemplify his method and possibly explain the translator's weariness of his approach:

> As regards the mode of the crucifixion there is now scarcely any debated point, if we except the question, whether the feet as well as the hands were nailed to the cross. As it lay in the interest of the orthodox view to prove the affirmative: so it was equally important to the rationalistic system to maintain the negative. . . . To the rationalists, on the contrary, it is at once more easy to explain the death of Jesus as a merely apparent death, and only possible to conceive how he could walk immediately after the resurrection, when it is supposed that his feet were left unwounded: but the case should rather be stated thus: if the historical evidence go to prove that the feet also of Jesus were nailed, it must be concluded that the resuscitation and the power of walking shortly after, either happened supernaturally or not at all. (Strauss 1846, III, 255–56)

The work of art Marian Evans turned to in order to escape Strauss' erudite fragmentations was Thorvaldsen's figure of the risen Christ, which was placed in front of her in her study at Foleshill (Laski 1973, 30). In many respects the translator thus shared the objections of Strauss' reviewers and was convinced that 'the million' would not enjoy Strauss (*GE Letters*, I, 185). Her doubts about *Das Leben Jesu* are further expressed in the belief that she was 'never pained' when Strauss was right, but that in many cases she considered him to be wrong (*GE Letters*, I, 203). Even though she eventually gained pleasure from reading her own English version of the text because it was so 'klar und ideenvoll' she was also convinced she did not know one person who was likely to read the book through (*GE Letters*, I, 218). As a result, she felt there was a need for an abridgement of this monumental three-volume piece of scholarship and expressed her willingness to provide one. The plan, however, never materialized (*GE Letters*, I, 354). Despite all these hesitations about the work, despite the fact that at times the translation seemed like a 'soul-stupefying labour' to Marian Evans, she never lowered her high standards of perfection and only very few instances of clear-cut errors have been traced (Martineau 1847, 162; *GE Letters*, I, 185). Even in the crucifixion passage quoted above she proved to be an assiduous judge of stylistic nuances in the German text and remained entirely committed to producing a faithful reproduction of the original. In addition, she expressed the determined wish to correct her proofs when questions of fidelity were at stake at a time when she must have been extremely pleased to see the end of her project (*GE Letters*, I, 198).

On the one hand, it must thus be conceded that Marian Evans was not fully in favour of the work which used up such a great deal of time and energy, and one could argue with Basil Willey that in terms of her own personal development Strauss 'could do little for her that Hennell had not already done' (Willey 1973, 230). On the other hand, it is not fair to diminish her efforts by describing them as 'an instance of feminine logic', as a critical reviewer of Cross' George Eliot biography attempted in the following passage:

> Indeed the whole book shows how impressionable, how emotional, how illogical, how feminine she was. In an Evangelical *milieu* she was strongly Evangelical. Transferred to the little Freethinking coterie of Hennells, Brays, Brabants, &c., she exchanged the matter of her evangelicism for unbelief, retaining its manner. It will probably provoke screams from her admirers, but we say hardly that if at the time when she fell under Lewes's male influence she had fallen under the male influence of an orthodox Churchman she would probably have been a pillar of the faith and a brand plucked from the burning. The person whom superficial critics long took to be the most masculine of her sex was a very woman. (Anon. 1885, 487)

After all, Marian Evans had agreed to become the translator of a text which had caused a sensation all over Europe and which was denounced as being part of the radical left-wing Hegelian movement (Alexander 1847, 257–58). It may have been the radicalism of the work which even led to the publication of a cheap English people's edition of *Das Leben Jesu* for the working class of Birmingham in 1842. The translation was considered to be mediocre and there is no evidence that Marian Evans was aware of its existence (Anon. 1846b, 269). Nevertheless, she did not wish to distance herself from the outrage the work created, and her rendering of Strauss' treatise into English thus turned into more than an arbitrary occupation triggered by her involvement in the circles of the Brays, Hennells and Brabants (Haight 1968, 68). As a result, her decision to depart from her family's evangelical convictions and to abstain from attending church had a strong intellectual foundation, which cannot seriously be called into question simply by the fact that she felt the need to recreate what Strauss 'un-created' by looking at

Thorvaldsen's sculpture at Foleshill while preparing Strauss' work for the general public.

What is more, Strauss was only the first in a series of questioning theologians Marian Evans chose to render into English. Her vow never to translate again after she had finished *The Life of Jesus* did not last long – three years later she was already engaged in the translation of Spinoza's *Tractatus Theologico-Politicus*, which never appeared in printed form (*GE Letters*, I, 280, 321). She had probably started work on this project in 1843, when her English renderings of foreign texts were considered to be too literal and did not yet give the impression of ease she conveyed in *The Life of Jesus*. As a result, her friend Mrs Bray was convinced that she could understand Spinoza's Latin better than the translator's English (*GE Letters*, I, 158). When Marian Evans eventually resumed her work on Spinoza in 1849 she returned to translation because she needed a 'rest to her mind' while looking after her dying father (*GE Letters*, I, 280; Redinger 1976, 151).

In December 1853 Ludwig Feuerbach's *Das Wesen des Christentums* was begun and the translator thus associated herself with a second sensational and possibly even scandalous German theological work of her own time. George Henry Lewes announced in *The Leader* that Feuerbach was a 'bombshell thrown into the camp of orthodoxy' (*GE Letters*, II, 165), and James Martineau commented on the publication of the book,

> It is a sign of 'progress,' we presume, that the lady-translator who maintained the anonymous in introducing Strauss, puts her name in the title-page of Feuerbach. She has executed her task even better than before: we are only surprised that, if she wished to exhibit the new Hegelian Atheism to English readers, she should select a work of the year 1840, and of quite secondary philosophical repute in its own country. (Martineau 1854, 559)

The accuracy of Martineau's depiction concerning the Feuerbach reception on the Continent is questionable. It is true that Feuerbach in the long run did not have the massive sceptical impact of Kant, Hegel, Marx or Nietzsche. Nevertheless, his work was considered to be explosive food for thought and exercised a great deal of influence on the philosophical and political scene of the time, including on the revolutionary upheavals of 1848 and the radical writings of Karl Marx (Harvey 1995, 6, 9). In England in contrast his ideas did not fall on fertile ground and Marian Evans' translation of his work was not read and discussed as widely as her rendering of Strauss' *Das Leben Jesu.*[5] Even though Feuerbach's treatise was in many ways more suited to a readership beyond the limited circle of academic theologians than Strauss' book, the negative response among her own countrymen did not come as a surprise to the translator. In January 1854, while she was still busy rendering the text into English, she wrote the following to Sara Hennell whose linguistic advice and proof-reading services she had managed to gain again:

> Your impression of the book exactly corresponds to its effect in Germany. It is considered *the* book of the age there, but Germany and England are *two* countries. People here are as slow to be set on fire as a *stomach*. Then there are the reviewers, who set up a mound of stupidity and unconscientiousness between every really new book and the public. Still I think the really wise and only dignified course for Mr. Chapman would be to publish it in his *Series* as he has announced it. (*GE Letters*, II, 137)

The change in attitude between the two translations from the German is obvious. In the case of Feuerbach Marian Evans approved of the work she chose to render into English in the main (*GE Letters*, II, 153). She agreed wholeheartedly with the theologian's concept of a religion of humanity, a man-centred form of spirituality following the principle that 'Man makes God in his own image' as opposed to 'God made man in his own image' (Martineau 1854, 559). The concept of God was thus treated as a projection of human rather than divine values and could be detached from any form of traditional church worship. As a result, Christian doctrines became a form of anthropology and sacraments were turned into human rather than divine concepts. James Martineau expressed his outrage about this notion in the following manner:

> The doctrine of Feuerbach receives an application at the close of the rites of baptism and the eucharist, which has been justly and universally condemned in Germany, and which the translator would have consulted his reputation by omitting. He professes to interpret the mystery of these two sacraments. Baptism means to say, that men,

[5] Apart from G.H. Lewes' and James Martineau's notices in *The Leader* and the *Westminster Review*, a short anonymous condemnation of the work can be found in the *Prospective Review* in 1854. For the neglect of Feuerbach in England see also Pfeiffer 1925, 255–56.

infants and all, cannot keep clean without washing; and the eucharist, that flour would be raw without the baker, and grapes crude without the winegrower! 'If in water, we declare – Man can do nothing without nature; by bread and wine we declare – Nature needs man, as man needs nature.' (Martineau 1854, 560)

As a matter of fact, Martineau's suggestion to omit passages and thus to amend the German text was observed by the translator at various points of the work, but not for the motives he would have liked to see. Marian Evans did indeed reconsider her own translation style, not with a view to concealing any of Feuerbach's ideas, but to making his philosophy more palatable for English readers. As a result, she showed more willingness than in the translation of Strauss to compromise her own high standards of faithfulness to the original text. In a letter to Sara Hennell she gave the following explanation for her decision:

I don't think a translator is bound to reproduce the *occasional* offensive defects of taste in a writer. I confess I have not gone on that principle of damaging faithfulness. Indeed I have felt it necessary in the part you have read to omit a whole sentence. I *could not* do otherwise – and indeed German sarcasm may be fairly said to be untranslateable. (*GE Letters*, II, 142)

The part Marian Evans is referring to at this point is Feuerbach's preface, which in her English rendering of the text significantly begins with a footnote stating that the 'opening paragraphs of this Preface are omitted, as having too specific a reference to transient German polemics to interest the English reader' (Feuerbach 1957, XXXIII). A letter to Sara Hennell includes further observations about Feuerbach's style and ways to improve it:

I shall send you Feuerbach's Preface soon. I wish you could have the German at the same time to amuse you. It is very curious that while his text is – *for a German* – concise, lucid and even epigrammatic now and then, his Preface reads like a caricature of the faults of German writing generally, one sentence is nearly a page and a half long! I have done my best to save this form appearing in the English, but I wish you to pay particular attention to the Preface and to mark everything which seems odd and does not flow easily – as it is very important that this preface *should be read*. (*GE Letters*, II, 140–41)

Similar considerations almost led Marian Evans to omit the second, third and fourth section of the appendix because she considered them to be 'abstract and Germanized "to a degree" ' and thought they 'might repel the reader from the appendix, which contains a great deal of important and accessible matter' (GE Letters, II, 154). In the end she retained most of these sections in her translation, but it cannot be denied that she was prepared to exercise an influence on the content of the German work, in order to improve its chances of a favourable reception in England. Probably out of personal enthusiasm for Feuerbach's philosophy Marian Evans was thus willing to act with a degree of independence from the original text which she would never have dared to employ in the case of Strauss.

What, then, spurred her interest in a work which caused a considerable measure of theological and political upheaval on the Continent and which was barely noted in the English periodical press? Interestingly enough, Feuerbach used terminology in defining the goals of his work which was very similar to that of Strauss:

Now that I have thus verified my analysis by historical proofs, it is to be hoped that readers whose eyes are not sealed will be convinced and will admit, even though reluctantly, that my work contains a faithful, correct translation of the Christian religion out of the Oriental language of imagery into plain speech. And it has no pretension to be anything more than a close translation, or, to speak literally, an empirical or historico-philosophical analysis, a solution of the enigma of the Christian religion. (Feuerbach 1957, XXXIII)

Translating sacraments into everyday life and thus detaching them from an ecclesiastical context, as well as making the supernatural elements of a religion part of a historically traceable world centred on human needs, were ideas which had a great attraction for Marian Evans at the time when she translated Feuerbach's Essence. In many respects, Feuerbach formulated conclusions to which his English translator had come in her own life. He offered her what was in many ways an 'un-German' a posteriori system with strong roots in real life, as opposed to an abstract philosophical framework obscured by church doctrines without tangible implications in the everyday world (Feuerbach 1957, XXXIII; GE 1855a, 151; Ashton 1994, 160). Feuerbach thus reconfirmed decisions she had made independently about her own religious convictions and provided her, as well some of her fictional heroines later, with an alternative and anthropomorphized ethical framework. In addition, he offered her a secular form of spirituality, which she used in order to reject the ideas of her own evangelical upbringing in a review of the work of Dr Cumming. In connection with this article which appeared anonymously in the *Westminster Review* in 1855 Marian Evans stated once again that she did not wish her gender to be revealed because the 'article appears to have produced a strong impression and that impression would be a little counteracted if the author were known to be a *woman . . .*' (GE 1855b, 158).

A few months before the publication of this review, which convinced George Henry Lewes that there was genius in its author, Marian Evans started her last substantial independent translation project: an English rendering of Spinoza's *Ethics* from the Latin. Owing to tensions between Lewes and the publisher Henry George Bohn this work was not printed during her lifetime (Ashton 1991, 174–76). Marian Evans' choice of translating the *Ethics* can be seen as a systematic continuation of work in a field which obviously preoccupied her mind at this stage of her life. George Henry Lewes drew a clear line between Spinoza and the German biblical criticism of his own day, in that Spinoza anticipated 'the rationalism of modern Germans', 'undertook a criticism of the Bible, and attacked the institution of priesthood as injurious to the general welfare' (Lewes 1843, 380).

The English rendering of Spinoza's *Ethics*, which was completed in 1856, marks the end of what Leslie Stephen described as George Eliot's protracted 'Pythagorean probation of silence'. It is significant that even as a novelist working under the male pseudonym George Eliot continued to write anonymous reviews, while she abandoned translating altogether. As a result, she reinforced the impression that there is a clear separation between her life as a translator and her life as a novelist. The following comparison between George Eliot's and Joseph Conrad's biography in F.R. Leavis' *The Great Tradition* is illuminating for our context:

> What can, nevertheless, be said, with obvious truth, is that Conrad is more completely an artist. It is not that he had no intellectual career outside his art – that he did nothing comparable to translating Strauss, Spinoza and Feuerbach, and editing *The Westminster Review*. It is that he transmutes more completely into the created work the interests he brings in. (Leavis 1973, 31–32)

This passage once again raises the question to what extent Marian Evans' translating and reviewing activities can be perceived as an intellectual career 'outside' and thus separated from what Leavis considered to be her genuinely artistic career as a novelist.

Marian Evans' most elaborate comment on this question was published in a review of J.M.D. Meiklejohn's rendering of Kant's *Critique of Pure Reason* and Mary Anne Burt's choice of specimens of the most celebrated German poets in 1855, one year before she gave up translating (GE 1855, 207–11). Even though this piece, which is entitled 'Translations and Translators', can be considered to be the most comprehensive theoretical tribute she paid to her own career as a translator, it did not exceed two printed pages in *The Leader*. A selection of the points discussed in the essay are worth highlighting for our purposes. Above all, Marian Evans insisted that translating required thorough professional training. The legend about the seventy translators, who were locked in separate cells by Ptolemy in order to turn the Old Testament into Greek and despite that came up with one unanimous version of the text, appeared to be an unduly idealistic perception of the task at stake to her. In this context she sarcastically recommended the motto ' "God helps them who help themselves" to all young ladies and some middle-aged gentlemen' who think they can replace a sound knowledge of their own as well as the foreign language they deal with by some form of 'supernatural aid' (Ibid. 1855, 208). This observation echoes the attitude she expressed in two 1846 letters to Sara Hennell in which she decided to send out clear signals of warning to Bradley Jenkins, one of her schoolfellows, who had considered becoming a professional translator:

A young lady of my acquaintance is so judicially blinded as to think translation and nothing but translation would be an easier life than that of a governess. She has asked me if it be possible for a person to get regular employment in this way. I do not suppose any scheme of the kind is practicable, and so I told her, but I promised to enquire for her. Her idea is that she could live in London and get her bread by turning German and French into English from morning to night. I wish you would be so good as to get a decided verdict against any such plan from an authoritative quarter that I might get the maggot out of her brain. (GE *Letters*, I, 212–13)

I shall tell her that I have asked the opinion of one friend, who thinks the speculation höchst precär, and shall I not say that that friend has had experience which warrants her to pronounce teaching better work for the soul than translating? There are not even the devil's wages for a translator – profit and fame. She says she wants neither, but only food and clothing. (GE *Letters*, I, 215)

J.M.D. Meiklejohn managed to live up to the high professional standards Marian Evans required, even though she considered Kant's *Critique of Pure Reason* to be 'perhaps the very hardest nut – the peachstone – for a translator to crack' (GE 1855c, 208). Mary Anne Burt's English rendering of German lyric poetry, on the other hand, was perceived to be less successful and caused Marian Evans to comment on the feasibility of poetic translations:

> A version like this bears about the same relation to the original as the portraits in an illustrated newspaper bear to the living face of the distinguished gentleman they misrepresent; and considering how often we hear opinions delivered on foreign poets by people who only know those poets at second hand, it becomes the reviewer's duty to insist again and again on the inadequacy of poetic translations.
>
> (Ibid., 209)

In the context of poetic translation she also observed that the Germans were better at translating foreign poetry than the English because 'their language, as slow and unwieldly as their own post-horses in prose, becomes in poetry graceful and strong and flexible as an Arabian war horse' (Ibid., 210). Even though she admired Schlegel's genius and his faithful adherence to the original text in his Shakespeare translations, Marian Evans felt the need to draw her readers' attention to the fact that the German could never be more than a feeble echo of the English original. After having discussed some mistakes the translators made she concluded her review with the following observation:

> Such examples of translators' fallibility in men like Schlegel and Tieck might well make less accomplished persons more backward in undertaking the translation of great poems, and by showing the difficulty of the translator's task, might make it an object of ambition to real ability. Though a good translator is infinitely below the man who produces *good* original works, he is infinitely above the man who produces *feeble* original works. We had meant to say something of the moral qualities especially demanded in the translator – the patience, the rigid fidelity, and the sense of responsibility in interpreting another man's mind. But we have gossiped on this subject long enough. (Ibid., 211)

The review in *The Leader* in many ways marked Marian Evans' departure from her life as a translator and summarized the mixed feelings she had accumulated about this activity by the time she abandoned it. On the one hand, she paid a great deal of respect to the

high level of training required for the provision of good translations
and acknowledged the severe difficulties inherent in the task. On the
other hand, she described her own comments as gossip and dedicated
no more than two printed pages to a theoretical evaluation of what had
been her main occupation for over a decade. In addition, she actively
tried to deter other people from becoming translators and expressed her
frustration about a lack of achievement during the 'translation period'
of her life. When she started her work on Strauss she went as far as to
ridicule her own efforts:

> It is very laughable that the I should be irritated about a thing in
> itself so trifling as a translation, but it is the very triviality of the thing
> that makes delays provoking. The difficulties that attend a really
> grand undertaking are to be borne, but things should run smoothly
> and fast when they are not important enough to demand the sacrifice
> of one's whole soul. (GE Letters, I, 191)

This attitude also prevailed while she was translating Feuerbach when
she complained about her own 'despair of achieving anything worth
the doing' (GE Letters, II, 156).

In her obituary note for George Eliot, her close friend Edith Simcox
pointed out that the author at all times 'regarded translation as a work
that should be undertaken as a duty, to make accessible any book that
required to be read' (1881, 780). Is it, then, a justifiable conclusion to
depict Marian Evans' translation efforts as a purposeless burden in her
life or an obstacle she had to overcome in order to write novels? It
cannot be denied that a number of her comments on the topic suggest
this conclusion. On the other hand, her translations and her ability to
read foreign texts in many respects served as a literary apprenticeship,
which familiarized her with the commercial aspects of the London
publishing scene. When the publication of her Strauss translation was
in danger of falling through, she considered covering the printing costs
off her own means (GE Letters, I, 190–91). In the end, her arduous
labour for Chapman was remunerated with twenty pounds and twenty-
five copies of the book itself. For the translation of Feuerbach she
received fifty pounds, but because the work was very unpopular with
the British public it turned out to be a heavy loss for the publisher (Call
1881, 160). Apart from introducing her to a business environment,
Marian Evans' extensive reception of foreign texts also shaped the
creativity she conveyed in her novels (McCobb 1982). After all,
Edward Casaubon's scholarship and possibly his marriage would have

had a greater chance of surviving if he, like the author of *Middlemarch*, had been able to read Max Müller's mythological research before immersing himself in what turned out to be an entirely superfluous project (GE 1987, 240; Stephen 1881, 480). In addition, it has been pointed out that in translating Feuerbach, 'Eliot was weaving her own tapestry for the future, a kind of Penelope spinning out a verbal plan' (Karl 1995, 166), and Feuerbach's framework of ethics has frequently been considered to be reflected in a number of her novels including *Adam Bede* and *Romola*.

On a biographical level it is her familiarity with Feuerbach's ideas which made it morally possible for her to develop an indifference towards the sanctions of religion and to disregard 'not the moral obligations of marriage, but the social law of England' in her relationship with George Henry Lewes (Acton 1885, 476; GE 1855b, 186). Ironically, one could argue that it is her translation activity which saved her from the gloomy future she envisaged for herself at the beginning of her literary life: fulfilling the duties of a mere 'literary secretary' as the wife of a dull German professor without having a career in her own right. What is more, her three major translations can be perceived as a coherent thematic unit dealing with questions which were crucial to her own intellectual development. While Strauss' *Das Leben Jesu* may not have been the text of Marian Evans' choice, it was her independent, free decision to render Feuerbach into English and to have her real name Marian Evans printed on the title-page of the book. What is more, her assertiveness as a translator grew and her rendering of Feuerbach as opposed to that of Strauss is no longer a faithful reproduction of 'word for word, thought for thought and sentence for sentence' (Anon. 1846a, 479). The translator now felt the need to point it out to Sara Hennell when she provided 'the raw Feuerbach, not any of her cooking' and chose to 'edit' the original text before rendering it into Engish in order to make it more attractive to the readership of her own country (*GE Letters*, II, 153). She may not have succeeded in achieving this goal, but her intention to break out of the anonymity and silence that surrounded her literary achievements cannot be denied. In retrospect Marian Evans' translations thus fulfilled a crucial and indispensable purpose in her literary development, for without them she would have been unlikely to develop into George Eliot, the novelist, and might never have produced the pieces of fiction which are associated with this name.

Works Cited

Acton, John Edward Emerich, 1885. 'George Eliot's "Life" ', *The Nineteenth Century* 17, 464–85.

[Alexander, Lindsay], 1847. 'Strauss's Life of Jesus', *British Quarterly Review* 5, 206–64.

[Allardyce, Alexander], 1881. 'George Eliot', *Blackwood's Magazine* 129, 255–68.

Anon., 1846a. 'Strauss's Life of Jesus', *Prospective Review* 2, 479–520.

Anon., 1846b. 'Strauss' Leben Jesu', *Dublin University Magazine* 28, 268–84.

Anon., 1854. 'Feuerbach's Essence of Christianity', *Prospective Review* 10, 581–84.

Anon., 1885. 'A too serious life', rpt. in Carroll (ed.), 1971, 484–89.

Ashton, Rosemary, 1994 (1980). *The German Idea*, London: Libris.

———, 1991. *G.H. Lewes. A Life*, Oxford: Clarendon Press.

Blind, Mathilde, 1883. *George Eliot*, London: W. H. Allen and Co.

Browning, Oscar, 1890. *Life of George Eliot*, London: Walter Scott.

[Call, W.M.W.], 1881. 'George Eliot: Her Life and Writings', *Westminster Review* n.s. 60, 154–98.

Carroll, David (ed.), 1971. *George Eliot. The Critical Heritage*, London: Routledge & Kegan Paul.

Cross, J.W., 1884. *George Eliot's Life*, 3 vols, Edinburgh and London: William Blackwood and Sons.

[Eliot, George], 'The Progress of the Intellect', rpt. in Pinney (ed.), 1963, 27–45.

[———], 1854. 'Woman in France: Madame de Sablé', rpt. in Pinney (ed.), 1963, 52–81.

[———], 1855a. 'The Future of German Philosophy', rpt. in Pinney (ed.), 1963, 148–53.

[———], 1855b. 'Evangelical Teaching: Dr Cumming', rpt. in Pinney (ed.), 1963, 158–89.

[———], 1855c. 'Translations and Translators', rpt. in Pinney (ed.), 1963, 207–11.

———, 1987 (1871–1872). *Middlemarch*, Harmondsworth: Penguin.

Feuerbach, Ludwig, 1957 (1841). *The Essence of Christianity*, trans. by George Eliot, New York, Evanston and London: Harper & Row, Publishers.

Haight, Gordon S. (ed.), 1954–1978. *The George Eliot Letters*, 9 vols, London: Oxford University Press.

———, 1968. *George Eliot. A Biography*, Oxford: Clarendon Press.

Harris, Horton, 1973. *David Friedrich Strauss and his Theology*, Cambridge: Cambridge University Press.

Harvey, Van A., 1995. *Feuerbach and the Interpretation of Religion*, Cambridge: Cambridge University Press.

James, Henry, 1885. 'George Eliot's Life', rpt. in Carroll (ed.), 1971, 490–504.

Karl, Frederick, 1995. *George Eliot. A Biography*, London: Harper Collins.

Laski, Margharita, 1973. *George Eliot and her world*, London: Thames and Hudson.

Leavis, F.R., 1973 (1960). *The Great Tradition*, London: Chatto & Windus.

[Lewes, George Henry], 1843. 'Spinoza's Life and Works', *Westminster Review* 39, 372–407.

———, 1968 (1855). *The Life and Works of Goethe*, London: Everyman.

[Martineau, James], 1847. 'Strauss and Parker', *Westminster Review* 47, 136–74.

[———], 1854. 'Contemporary Literature', *Westminster Review* 62 o.s., 559–60.

McCobb, Anthony, 1982. *George Eliot's Knowledge of German Life and Letters*, Salzburg: Institut für Anglistik und Amerikanistik.

Pfeiffer, Sibilla, 1925. *George Eliots Beziehungen zu Deutschland*, Heidelberg: Carl Winter's Universitätsbuchhandlung.

Pinney, Thomas (ed.), 1963. *Essays of George Eliot*, London: Routledge and Kegan Paul.

Prickett, Stephen, 1991. 'Romantics and Victorians: from Typology to Symbolism', in Prickett (ed.), *Reading the Text. Biblical Criticism and Literary Theory*, Oxford: Blackwell, 182–224.

Redinger, Ruby V., 1976. *George Eliot. The Emergent Self*, London, Sydney, Toronto: The Bodley Head.

Simcox, Edith, 1881. 'George Eliot', *The Nineteenth Century* 9, 778–801.

Spinoza, Benedict Baruch, 1981 (1677). *Ethics*, trans. by George Eliot, ed. by Thomas Deegan, Salzburg: Institut für Anglistik und Amerikanistik.

[Stephen, Leslie], 1881. 'George Eliot', rpt. in Carroll (ed.), 1971, 464–84.

Strauss, David Friedrich, 1846 (1835). *The Life of Jesus*, 3 vols, London: Chapman.

———, 1973 (1835). *The Life of Jesus Critically Examined*, London: SCM Press Ltd.

Willey, Basil 1973 (1949). *Nineteenth-Century Studies. Coleridge to Matthew Arnold*, Harmondsworth: Penguin.

Notes on Contributors

Susan Bassnett is professor of Comparative Cultural Studies at the University of Warwick, where she teaches Translation Studies at post-graduate level. She is the editor of two major series of volumes on translation (the Routledge Translation Studies series and the Multilingual Matters Topics in Translation series). Her books include *Translation Studies* (Routledge 1991) and *Comparative Literature: A Critical Introduction* (Blackwell 1993). She has translated novels, plays and poetry from Latin, Spanish, French, Italian and Polish.

John Corbett lectures in English Language at Glasgow University, and contributes to Cultural Studies seminars within and outwith the UK. He is the author of *Language and Scottish Literature* (Edinburgh University Press, 1997).

Theo Hermans read Germanic languages at Ghent University (Belgium), literary translation at Essex and Comparative Literature at Warwick. He is now professor of Dutch and Comparative Literature at University College London. His research interests include translation theory and history, and Renaissance and modern Dutch literature. Among his publications in English are *The Flemish Movement* (ed., 1992), *The Manipulation of Literature* (ed., 1985) and translations of poems by Hugo Claus and H.C. ten Berge.

Piotr Kuhiwczak is Director of the Centre for British and Comparative Cultural Studies, University of Warwick. He studied comparative literature and literary translation at Warsaw University and wrote his doctoral thesis on Byron's reception in Poland. He is the author of numerous articles on translation theory and history and has translated between Polish and English. His latest book is *Successful Polish-English Translation*. His current project is a Translation Studies Reader.

André Lefevere (1945–1996) was Professor of Germanic Languages at the University of Texas at Austin. He was one of the founders of the new interdiscipline of Translation Studies, and author of numerous books and articles. Among his best-known works are *Translating Poetry: Seven Strategies and a Blueprint* (Van Gorcum, 1975), *Translation/History/Culture: A sourcebook* (Routledge, 1992), *Translation, Rewriting and the Manipulation of Literary Fame* (Routledge, 1993).

Felicity Rosslyn is Senior Lecturer at the University of Leicester. She studied literary translation at Cambridge and Harvard and wrote her doctoral thesis on Pope's *Iliad*. She is the author of numerous articles on translations from the Classics and also from Russian, Polish, and Yugoslav literature. She edits *The Cambridge Quarterly* and her latest book is *Alexander Pope: A Literary Life*. Her current project is a 'translation' of the plots of Greek tragedy into modern terms.

Susanne Stark is a University Research Fellow in the German Department at Leeds. She has published articles in her research interests, which include the historical and cultural context of translation, Anglo-German literary relations, as well as nineteenth- and twentieth-century women writers. She is currently finishing a book entitled *'Behind Inverted Commas'. Translation and Anglo-German Cultural Relations in the Nineteenth Century*.